The 30 D's of Greatness

Greatness

(A Step by Step Guide for Success and Greatness)

By Jason M. Smith

Title: The 30 D's of Greatness
Subtitle: A Step by Step Guide for Success and Greatness

Edited by Jaquon C. Heath

ISBN: 9781731246219

Table of Contents

How I Got The Idea   4

0. What is Greatness?   12

1. Discovery   17

2. Dream   28

3. Different   37

4. Design   43

5. Detail   52

6. Direction   61

7. Decision   69

8. Declare   80

9. Dare   89

10. Deliberate   96

11. Do   103

12. Desire   117

13. Drive   121

14. Defiance   133

15. Diligence   141

16. Dedication   147

17. Determination   153

18. Devotion   159

19. Desperate   165

20. Defeat   174

21. Deep   184

22. Deal   193

23. Demand   203

24. Develop   210

25. Define   216

26. Discipline   223

27. Dominate   232

28. Dictate   241

29. Divinity   248

30. Destiny   253

Index   257

How I Got The Idea

You may think this book is about success, but that's a false depiction. Actually it's about failure. So if this book is not for you, do not waste your time. We do not run away from failure in this book. We run towards it with a smile, because success in life always begins with **failure.**

My coworker, Rich, asked me if I wanted to do a line of coke with him before we got the day started; "It'll keep you focused," he said. I respectfully declined, I had other ways of focusing—like thinking about the people I loved or the things I wanted to buy. Rich and I had some good memories though—clubs, girls, rolexes, and big deals, but I didn't need another addiction in my life, success was my only one.

The *Wolf of Wall Street* lifestyle was what I wanted, not all the drugs, but some of the fun. I wanted the prosperity, the power, and the luxury; all things I dreamed of as a gullible kid.

The Stock Broker Life

The stock broker life in the early 2000's was like trying to relive the 90's. We didn't have the Lamborghinis and Ferraris in the movie *Boiler Room*, but we were doing okay with our BMWs and Benzes. Becoming an instant millionaire was far from reality, but I had an opportunity to become a thousandaire, so that was my main goal.

I had gotten far from humble beginnings; I graduated from college and sealed a good job as a stockbroker. Now all I had to do was reel in some big bucks and I'd be living my dream life, right? Maybe.

Some days were better than others, some of my checks were average, others were above average, but I wasn't a thousandaire yet—I was missing the right formula. Since I was always busy with work, I didn't think I had time to seek out the "right" formula. I just knew that making these calls would somehow pay off.

On December 15, 2005 my life changed. Before this day, I wasn't where I wanted to be, but I was doing okay. I reminded myself that I had a nice 2002 GMC Envoy, a home, and a supportive girlfriend. Motivated by positivity, I fired up my computer at work, went over a few voice exercises, brought the telephone close to me, and started dialing at 8:30 a.m.

Even though I used my Glenn Gary lead cards (those are the best leads) and told my co-workers to ABC—Always Be Closing—my calls that morning were crap and my coffee wasn't strong enough to wake me up. I didn't put enough effort in my sales pitches that morning; maybe I was too hung over from the night before or my coffee wasn't strong enough, but I figured I'd **d**o better after lunch.

As soon as I got out of my chair for a stretch, the CEO, James, called me into his office. He liked to give pep talks, he's similar to a football coach in that way. Usually, he calls me in once a week to go over the same routine: "Don't you want to take your girlfriend to nice restaurants? Don't you want to buy a nice house, car, and anything you desire? Don't you want to be rich like me?" and the final closer, "Don't you want to make your family proud?"

Of course I wanted those things, and I wanted them sooner than later, but hearing him say them time and time again was tiring. Yet, I still had to put on a nice face while preparing myself for the pep talk. I walked into his office with a fake burst of energy; he gave a wide grin and gestured me to sit down. He calmly looked at me; I could tell he'd been thinking about this for some time. Then he said, "Jay, I want you to know that you are my Pete Rose—my grinder! He was one of the best hitters in his day, and you are one of my best brokers."

I wasn't prepared for this, I think I actually gestured my head back with a confused face, and I stuttered a bit as I thought about his reason for complimenting me—in the stock business, you had to be careful of who you trusted and what angle they were coming from. "Thank you," I responded as I cleared my throat. Then he asked me a serious question, "have you heard of the four Ds of success?"

The four Ds were on his wall which was behind me as I sat facing him, and I saw them every time I passed his office, but at that moment, I could only think of 3. Confidently, I answered, " **d**edication, **d**etermination, and **d**rive." I wasn't sure about the last one, so he told me it was **d**esire.

"Jay, this is how I became rich and successful at life. I had the desire to win, I was determined to win, I was dedicated to my goals, and I drove myself every day." He had my attention now. Half of me felt like I knew this, the other half felt like I just learned something new. Honestly, the words themselves didn't affect me, they were all words I've used before, but it was the possible manifestation of these words that gave me the chills. It was one of those 'mind blowing' moments. I used to be careless with words, I used them for normal conversation like anyone else; but at that moment, he put them under a microscope where the words were no longer immaterial. They became concrete things that I could touch and understand. It was the difference between a road signal and the small, intricate wires within the signal that made it blink.

The Ds

"Determination" was just a word, but there were small, intricate wires in that word that made it blink. In order for me to understand determination, I had to clearly define it. So I had to say, "determination is the will to keep going no matter how difficult the obstacle or circumstance." Then, after I defined it, I created a design for how I would achieve it, a blueprint.

My thoughts went on in this pattern, one D came after the other. My boss said a few more things to me, but they barely registered. "You get me Jay?" He asked. "Huh?" I broke out of my thoughts. "Yeah, yeah, of course, the right desire, I get it, yeah."

7

That afternoon, I left the office for lunch, but I fed on my thoughts. Instead of just letting my words be immaterial objects, they became concrete material objects and actions that manifested around me. I couldn't just say that I'd finish an assignment, but my existence depended on finishing the assignment. It was as if the words were spells spoken out of a wizard's mouth. I was the wizard, the **d**esigner of my own **d**estiny.

My desk felt **d**ifferent when I returned from lunch. My mind was refreshed. I hit the phones with more **d**etermination, and in-between calls, I thought **d**eeply about how I'd control the conversation. If a wealthy person gave my high-pitched, nasally voice a chance, I'd prove that I could make him or her a lot of money. I didn't speak immaterial words, but I casted spells. I closed a client that evening because I truly *felt* **d**etermined and **d**riven. It wasn't a one-hit-wonder close either because I went on to be one of the best closers in my firm.

I don't believe people just change. I believe certain events trigger change; I changed how I **d**efined my life thanks to the Ds. That morning, like most people, I was someone who used whatever words came to his mind. But that afternoon, I became someone who **d**eliberately used words. Now I **d**efine my life through the Ds, and I want to show you how to do so as well.

I used the Ds to get to where I am today: I am an accomplished entrepreneur, a family man, and in many respects, a rich man—socially, emotionally, mentally, and financially. Usually, I wouldn't give this information out, but I figured since I've already proven its validity, I might as well share it with you. I've read books on how to be successful throughout my life, and those authors helped me; I've also received plenty of in-person help along the way.

It's only right that I share my knowledge so you can learn as I have!

Qualities

Take a moment to write down on the next two blank pages the qualities you possess, both negative and positive. Leave a good amount of space between each quality because you will be adding 3-4 bullet points underneath each one.

Positive Qualities

Negative Qualities

<u>0. What is Greatness?</u>

You were born with potential. You were born with goodness and trust. You were born with ideals and dreams. You were born with greatness. You were born with wings. You are not meant for crawling, so don't. You have wings. Learn to use them and fly.—

Jalaluddin Rumi

Be Great

Thank you for completing the exercise. Before we move on, let's define greatness, just as we will define our lives. According to Webster's Dictionary, *great* is an extent, amount, or intensity considerably above the normal or average. Someone who is great does things far above the average. Just the other day, I read about a man named Johnny Strange who holds the Guinness World Record for carrying the heaviest amount (47lb 10oz) of weight with pierced ears. This may be a strange (pun intended) record to have, but average people cannot lift 47lbs with their ears, and only a small group of people will be able to break that record; so since Strange is so far from the average, he is great.

Consider a more common activity, like track. Jesse Owens, a historic athlete and icon, became the first U.S. athlete to win four track and field gold medals in under 45 minutes at an Olympic Game. This was in 1936 at the Berlin Olympic Games where certain groups, including Adolf Hitler's Nazi Party, believed that black people were inferior to whites. So Owens' victory showed both his own greatness and the greatness of the human spirit to defy adversity. His record remained unbroken for 48 years.

Everyone Has Greatness in Them

When thinking of great people, names like Usain Bolt, Michael Phelps, Oprah Winfrey, Elon Musk, and Steve Jobs come to mind. But what about Johanna Quaas, the senior citizen gymnast who completes somersaults in her 90's; or Carlton Williams, the builder who does 2,200 pushups in an hour; or Zhang Shuang, a man who can run 164 feet in 20.09 seconds on his hands with a soccer ball between his legs! These great people are not the usual celebrity types, and a lot of celebrities are not even great. People who are far above the average at what they do are great!

Fame does not make someone great. In our society, a lot of people believe that being famous equals greatness, but that's far from true. Nowadays, average people who **d**o nothing get famous, and great people who overcome tremendous feats sometimes go unrecognized; but when you are great, there is no limit. Your greatness can lead to fame and abundance if you want. However, fame does not last but greatness can stand the test of time. Greatness can be passed down to generations and it can lead to ultimate fulfillment in life--something no amount of fame or materials can offer.

Before we get into the D's, answer this question, what great people influence you? Now think of a few important traits these people possess that make them great. I'm sure some of them have traits like **d**irection, **d**evotion, **d**edication, and **d**esign. Throughout your life, you have heard and used these D's regularly in normal conversation, so you probably think you understand them, but the true meaning can only be understood in practice. So think about the actions these great and influential people carry out that show direction, devotion, dedication, design, and more.

There are three forces that influence your greatness.

1. First, there is you. Now is the time to put yourself under a microscope. Take a moment to answer this question, who are you? Be truthful. Throughout this book, you will be challenged to reflect on yourself, including the habits and qualities *you* currently possess and those you want.

2. The second force that influences your greatness is stimuli or triggers--people, nature, circumstance, family, and environment. You can understand more fully how these forces influence you as you continue reading.

3. Third, there is the vision of who and where you want to be. As you read this book, you'll be able to see through your mind's eye the end result, but for now, you must be humble and put yourself in the

beginning stage of your greatness—the **d**iscovery

stage.

You have to advance through five sequential stages to

greatness: The Discovery Stage, The Do Stage, The Defeat Stage,

The Development Stage, and The Destiny Stage. There are

important D's in each stage that you must learn in order to

understand and implement them in your daily life. Once you learn

to implement them, you can ultimately reach your **greatness**. Use

this book as a guide and re-read it if you ever find yourself in a

tight spot throughout your journey to greatness!

1. Discovery

Discovery consists of looking at the same thing as everyone else and thinking something different. - Albert Szent-Györgyi

Discover Yourself

The first exercise you wrote down at the beginning of this book should have helped you focus on each of your unique qualities. Now to **d**iscover yourself, take those qualities and elaborate on them. In order to **d**o that, you'll need to know what triggered them. A trigger is something that happens to you, but you don't have to act on it. You can receive triggers your entire life and never act on them. But the moment a trigger affects your senses and emotions so greatly that you react, your actions set the stage for habits that completely shape you, and you are never the same again. That moment is one of your decisive moments, where your life changes forever.

I once met a man who blew up with anger whenever he was annoyed. After we talked about his past, he realized that his anger dated back to his experiences with his mother who would often react with anger to small things. Those experiences with his mother influenced him to blow up with anger like she did whenever he was annoyed. These are the triggers you want to understand so you can react to them in healthy ways.

If you are hardworking, what motivates you to work hard? Can you pinpoint a specific time, place, or event that changed you forever? Did you lose a job? Fail an exam? Listen to a motivational speech? or something as simple as miss an opportunity to say I love you? All of these are triggers, but how did you react to them? When you lost your job, did you give up looking, or did you apply for new work. When you failed the exam, were you **d**efeated or did you **d**ecide to change your study habits; when you listened to that motivational speech, was there something in the speech that triggered a reaction from you; when you missed the opportunity to say "I love you," were you so hurt that you changed your affection for others?

These triggers rouse you, and they are a part of your self-**d**iscovery, but it is your reaction to them that shapes you into the person you become. **So take the time to review your list of qualities and on the right-hand side of or in bullet format underneath the qualities, write out each trigger that caused them and the reaction that changed your life forever.**

Example:

1. **Quality (characteristic):** Hustler
   - **Trigger Moment:** My family was in financial despair. My parents were stressed and panicking.
   - **Reaction:** Seeing my Mother crying made me so sad and angry that I started hustling jewelry with my brother in order to make money for our family.

***

After you complete the above exercise, it's time to parse through your trigger moments, one by one, and write out how they impact[ed] you negatively or positively throughout your life. **Before you continue reading this chapter, take a moment to write out the impacts and reflect on them. Write out the negative and/or positive impacts in bullet format underneath the reaction.**

1. **Quality (characteristic):** Hustler
   - **Trigger Moment:** My family was in financial despair. My parents were stressed and panicking.

- **Reaction:** Seeing my Mother crying made me so sad and angry that I started selling jewelry with my brother in order to make money for our family.
    - **Positive Impact:** This had a positive effect on me because I learned how to support myself and family at a young age.
    - **Negative Impact:** I became very angry and irritated with people.

When you are negatively impacted by negative triggers, you cease being your true *self*. When you are mad, you say rude things to nice people; when you are tired, you get lazy; when you are stressed, you act unreasonable. It's hard to be great at something when you are mad, sad, lazy, tired, unreasonable.

You certainly need negativity and positivity to motivate you, but you want to keep the negativity low. Too much negativity, like anger and hate, can result in regrettable actions. As you can guess, **d**iscovery is about reducing the negative energy, while increasing the positive energy; you want to learn more about the qualities you posses that make you happy and fulfilled. If the negativity in your life is greater than the positivity, you are holding too much of a burden to focus on your own greatness.

On your list of qualities and the triggers that cause them, highlight the positive qualities. Think about how you can be great at something by using and enhancing those qualities.

Sean "P.Diddy/Puff Daddy" Combs

In 1974, a 15 year old Sean[1] "Puff Daddy" Combs, the current multi-millionaire entrepreneur and record producer, asked his single parent mother for a new pair of Pro Keds sneakers. During that time these sneakers were in style, so all of the other kids were wearing them, but his mother couldn't afford them.

Combs was 2 years old when his father died in a drug deal gone wrong in Harlem. His mother didn't want her two children to fall into the same footsteps as their father, so she moved her family out of the hard streets of 1970s Harlem, New York, and into the more suburban town of Mount Vernon, New York. In order to pay the bills while supporting her family, she worked 3 - 4 jobs, which meant both her money and time were limited. So when she gave her son a look of disappointment and told him she was unable to

---

[1] Wolny, Philip. *Sean Combs*. Rosen Pub. Group, 2006.

buy the sneakers, it hurt him. That look of disappointment was imprinted in Combs' mind forever. This negative trigger produced a positive reaction in Combs, and it helped him discover his passion. At that moment, and for the rest of his life, he became a hustler.

He began looking for a job at 12 years old, but understandably, he couldn't find one. So he convinced some paperboys in his area to let him do their routes for a percentage, and he eventually ran a paperboy operation with 6 routes. After that initial trigger moment, his life was defined by the qualities of hard work, hustle, and enterprise.

Negative triggers are extremely powerful, but reactions don't only have to come from a place of pain. Among her other jobs, Sean's mother was a clothing designer; she would make sure Sean dressed in fancy outfits to model her clothing. Sean fell in love with that scene. He enjoyed entertainment and being the center of attention; and any chance he got, he made himself in the spotlight. It was a characteristic that followed him as he danced in parties and music videos. As his greatness grew, he eventually started his own fashion line because fashion is a way to gain attention.

He reacted to triggers in life by **d**eveloping strong qualities, like hustle, entertainment, and enterprise, which later led to his success as a dancer, music producer, and entrepreneur. Our reactions to triggers help us **d**iscover ourselves. What are your trigger moments?

My Experience

I grew up in a decent house with my brother in a respectable part of North Babylon, NY. Though I had both parents in my life as a child, circumstance threatened to send my family into dysfunction and misery. I learned this the hard way at age 12 when I found out my family was going through hard times and it would effect the way we lived. Can you imagine seeing your mother **d**esperately crying on the living room floor?

Some people might shy away from responsibility, grow weak from fear, and embrace hopelessness; but my brother and I chose a different path. Seeing my mother in a depressing state triggered a reaction out of me. At that moment, I decided to become a hustler, and I defined my life as a hustler ever since.

Hustler

A hustler is someone who works hard to earn money, a hustler won't take no for an answer, a hustler works on their aspirations day and night. I sold mixtapes, worked odd jobs, and started a jewelry business with my brother in order to develop the sales skills and drive of a hustler. That jewelry business didn't flourish, but we were able to provide for ourselves until our parents got back on their feet.

Ever since I decided to begin working, I was a hustler. That was the first part of my self-discovery—discovering the things that molded me into *me*. Since I was in sales, I could have identified myself as a salesman, but that was too limited of a definition for me. It didn't matter what I sold, I was a hustler.

Consequently, from that very day, I discovered that I liked helping others. The mental strength I exhibited to help my family was the same strength I used to help others. Now, I run a

successful ambulette company which directly helps others, and I

love what I do.

Get Rid of Phony

When trying to discover yourself, you must understand the positive

and negative triggers of your life that have influenced you. You

cannot fool yourself. Who you are *is* reality and it will not go

away no matter what people say about you, or what lies you tell

yourself. One problem people face when trying to discover

themselves is they pretend to be someone they are not, and they

build themselves around a false persona. That persona becomes so

ingrained in them that they lose a sense of self, and eventually they

self-destruct. You do not want to discover who you are while

allowing who you are not to weigh you down. If you do this, you

will create a dysfunction in your personality, which can cause

depression and misery. Let go of everything phony so you can

discover yourself without any setbacks.

Personally, I knew going to college was a stepping stone for me; I needed it in order to reach the position I wanted in life at that time. However, I didn't pretend to be someone I wasn't—I was not a good student. So yes, I did better in some classes than others, but I knew myself well enough to do just the bare minimum to attain my college degree.

Embrace Who You Are

If you loved playing with trinkets or you were always a "nerd" in school, do not lie and tell yourself that you are not a nerd now because you changed your appearance; embrace yourself. Bill Gates would not have become a billionaire if he didn't embrace his inner nerd, neither would Steve Jobs. These individuals had no problem being themselves; furthermore, their fascination with their own uniqueness and the production of their own inventions was greater than any lie.

My Hobbies

Fashion was one of my hobbies; I followed fashion trends in my neighborhood as a kid. But fashion was not one of Steve Job's hobbies. He was a man who couldn't miss a chance to wear old New Balance sneakers, blue jeans, and a black turtleneck sweater wherever he went. But that was *him*, and he wouldn't try to trick himself into believing he was someone else, and neither should you.

So to recap: First, review your qualities. Second, think about the triggers that caused decisive reactions in your life? Third, do not lie to yourself, be authentic.

2. Dream

Hold fast to dreams
For if dreams die
Life is a broken-winged bird
That cannot fly.
Hold fast to dreams
For when dreams go
Life is a barren field
Frozen with snow.

- Langston Hughes

Discovering yourself is the most consequential part of this process.

Scores of good people have gone down the wrong path in life just

because they didn't discover themselves. If you don't discover

yourself and go through this process, you *will* be lost; do not try to

fool yourself. Sure, you can easily put on a facade as if you're

living your dreams. You can smile wide in social media pictures

and go to cool places and take pictures with friends, but inside

you'll know that it's all fake; you'll know that you are just

pretending and hiding. You'll find yourself in a job that you don't

like, around people who don't value you, with responsibilities you don't want, and with problems that could've been avoided. Once

you **d**iscover yourself, you will have a foundation to build on.

You've known about **d**reams all of your life; maybe you

shied away from yours. Your childhood was filled with them, and

your imagination ran wild with them. You might have *dreamed* of

getting out of tough situations, of transforming yourself into

someone **d**ifferent, of being a champion, or of changing your

lifestyle; whatever your **d**ream was or is, now is the time to tap

into them!

It is a shame that as we get older, the fire of our **d**reams

dim. The most fortunate of us enjoy a childhood free from

responsibility and full of dreams. But when we get older, more

pressure is put on us; responsibility kicks in, and then our **d**reams

get put to the side. At those moments, our job is to put ourselves

back in the mindset of a child. We need to find moments— breaks

from work, right before we get out of bed in the morning or go to

sleep at night—where we can **d**ream. We have to understand that dreaming is healthy for the human soul, and if we're not dreaming, then we are being content with an unhealthy lifestyle.

Visualization

The secret to dreaming is visualization. First your **d**ream has to be honest and aligned with your self-discovery, then the visualization process can take effect. Only at the point where a clear **d**iscovery of self is aligned with a **d**ream will you be able to visualize what you truly want in life. If you **d**iscover that you are a history lover, then your **d**ream will be tied to that self-discovery, but it will be expressed in **d**ifferent ways from others. Maybe as a history lover, you **d**ream of working in museums, film, teaching, writing, antiquities collection, or vintage cars. The possibilities are endless. Your **d**ream will be unique to you.

Speaking of cars, I have always liked cars. And I dreamed of buying a new Mercedes Benz at one point in my life, but in order to make that **d**ream a reality, I had to visualize it. I visualized the new car, visualized myself going to the dealership, visualized how I would take the money out to pay for it, and visualized myself driving it. Actually, I put a picture of the SL550

Mercedes coupe on my ceiling, which I looked at every day. These

visualizations gave me an understanding of where I wanted to go

and how I could get there, so when the opportunity presented itself

for me to buy the car of my dreams, I knew how to take advantage

of it.

What is Your Dream?

So I ask you a simple question: What is your **d**ream? If your

dream seems impossible, it's okay. Imagine living in a world

where there is no such thing as humans flying airplanes. To the

inhabitants of this world, ground and ocean travel is the status quo

—it is everyday life. This was the case some two hundred years

ago; during the 1800's, airplanes were unthinkable. It was normal

for people to believe that the Wright Brothers' **d**ream was

impossible. But now we know it was very possible.

So think hard about what you want; be unabashedly

imaginative and impossible with your dreams. Honestly, the more

outlandish your **d**ream, the better. Dream about it so hard that it appears in your mind's eye as if it is happening right in front of you.

In 1959, a 5 year old Oprah Winfrey[2] was living on a farm in Mississippi with her grandmother. Her grandmother was a caretaker who taught young Oprah how to read by the age of three. Oprah was quoted as saying, "books were my pass to personal freedom…and [I] soon discovered there was a whole world to conquer that went beyond our farm in Mississippi."

Since opportunities were very scarce for black women in those days and care taking was a guaranteed job, her grandmother taught her about care taking. But that life wasn't for Oprah. Oprah dreamed of something greater for herself. She wanted to express herself, she wanted to be seen, she wanted to be an actress, she wanted to work in the communications world. And so she dreamed of these things long and hard, and sometimes her dreams would take hold of her while she was on the farm, and she'd find herself play acting in front of farm animals.

---

[2] Kelley, Kitty. *Oprah: a Biography*. Three Rivers Press, 2011.

Life took a turn for the worst when Oprah went to live with her 18 year old, unmarried mother. Her mother was too busy to give her the attention she needed, so oftentimes her mother entrusted her in the care of family members. Unfortunately, at the vulnerable age group of 9-14, various male family members took advantage of her by molesting and raping her. This abuse caused Oprah to lose her sense of self-worth. She saw herself as valueless, and she acted destructively.

Eventually, after she was rejected from a juvenile detention home at the age of 14, she went to live with her father in Tennessee. Staying with her father was a huge relief. Under her father's strict guidance, she thrived academically. Oprah even got the opportunity to speak and sing in her local church. After she earned $500.00 for a speaking engagement in church, she decided that getting paid to speak was her path. Having discovered herself, she began focusing on her dreams. She went on to win the Nashville Miss Fire Prevention Pageant in 1971, where she said she wanted to be a journalist like Barbara Walters. Later she won the Miss Black Tennessee Pageant, received a full scholarship to Tennessee State University, and became a news anchor for the WTVF-TV station at age 19—earning her place as the first black news anchor in Nashville's history.

Oprah dreamed of being paid to speak, dreamed of expressing herself to thousands of people, and dreamed of a career in media. At the young age of 5, she visualized her **d**ream to the point of acting out what she wanted. Although she went through traumatic experiences, she held on to her dreams and didn't let them go. Some important takeaways from Oprah's story are to align your dreams with your discovered self, to visualize, and to hold on to the dreams. Hardships are inevitable. But you have to hold on as if you are holding on to a cliff, and below is certain death. A lost dream can be worse than death, because you'll always wonder "what if?" while doing work that doesn't make you fulfilled.

Childhood Dreams

As far as I can remember, I always dreamed of being successful, and to a seven year old boy in the 80s, being successful meant having more money and potentially being rich. Even as a seven year old, I knew having more money would help my family be comfortable instead of pinching pennies; interestingly, I learned about this through my mom's favorite shows, like *The Cosby Show* and *Dallas*.

I don't know if it was my mother's love for these shows that spawned a love for them in me, but I was definitely intrigued by the lifestyles of J. R. Ewing, the C.E.O of Ewing Oil, and Dr. Huxtable, a Physician. But at seven years old, I didn't understand how they became wealthy, I just knew that I wanted that lifestyle.

One thing I did know at seven years old was that doctors and professional athletes made good money. So for many years, I dreamed of being a doctor, a professional football player, or a boxer. I envisioned myself as Dr. Huxtable from the Cosby's, or

Lawrence Taylor, the NFL player, or Iron Mike Tyson, my favorite boxer.

I held on to these dreams from childhood into my teenage years, but somewhere my dreams faded as reality kicked in. I didn't see many lawyers or doctors in my neighborhood; it was a blue collar neighborhood. So I didn't have much to hook me into the dream of being a doctor, however I still wanted a good lifestyle. I needed money, and my need for money turned into a desire for the stock broker life. In high school, I vowed to become rich to take care of my family, so that's the path I took. I didn't discover myself at this time because I was chasing money instead of my purpose in life, but I was taking the long route to discovery. I made good money as a stockbroker, but my life would have been *richer* if I had stuck to my dreams and discovered myself beforehand. **You can dream, but to bring that dream into fruition, you need much more than wishes and hopes; you need a plan, aka a design.**

3. Different

In order to be irreplaceable one must always be different.
- Coco Chanel

The Irony of Being Different

If everyone is the same, then no one can be great; your greatness is a product of your uniqueness--your differences from others. The irony of being **d**ifferent is that you are being yourself; you are not trying to be like anyone else. Your difference is connected to your choices, your characteristics, your experiences, and even your DNA. Unless you are a genetic twin, your DNA is substantially **d**ifferent from others, and your experiences in life are **d**ifferent from others as well. So why would you try to be someone else? Don't get it wrong, you can be inspired by other people, you can adopt some of the characteristics of other people, but you are your own unique individual. No one else on this earth has a combination of your appearance, style, interest, and experience. If you want to be great, then you must embrace your own uniqueness.

As social beings, we are wired to work together. Our brains contain mirror neurons which help us develop empathy and communicate effectively; these mirror neurons allow us to identify facial expressions, emotions, voices, and actions while imitating them. This is why the environment we grow up in greatly affects our uniqueness--we participate in the culture and experiences of the places we come from.

So a Haitian citizen from Port-au-Prince will most likely eat different foods and have a different accent than one from Carrefour, and both of them will have different customs and accents than a U.S. citizen from Florida. Your job as a unique individual is to break away from things in your environment that you disagree with or that don't interest you without breaking away from the culture that makes you unique. I am a black New Yorker, I appreciate and love my culture; wherever I go, I have the uniqueness of being a black New Yorker, but I will never be anyone's stereotype. I am a U.S. citizen; wherever I go, I have the uniqueness of being a U.S. citizen, but I disagree with certain viewpoints and I don't believe in many dominant national ideas.

I grew up with one brother, two loving parents, and a couple of cousins in my household. I embraced my parents and mentors, they helped me develop my character and greatly influenced me, but I didn't, and still don't, agree with all of their values or actions.

I make my own decisions and follow the values I believe in, whether those values are the ones my family shares or not. Embrace your uniqueness internationally, nationally, locally, and interpersonally. It's a sad day when you loses your uniqueness in life because that's the day identity crisis forms; without set values and a uniqueness to stand on, you can fall for any bad idea. You'll never be able to reach your greatness if you are easily swayed or if you have a fragmented sense of self.

If you have ever wondered why large groups of people are able to commit horrible acts of violence and injustice, understand that it's because of things like conformity, a lost sense of self, and cowardice from people who should know better. A famous psychology study by social psychologist Solomon Asch proved that humans have a conformity problem. The study included one test subject and eight fake ones. The real test subject was placed second to last in a row of nine participants. All of the subjects were asked the same questions and obliged to answer the questions out loud, one by one. Each time a question was given, the answer was so obvious that the real test subject knew it immediately. However, what happened when the study started was shocking. The first question was given, and the first test subject answered it incorrectly, the second gave the same incorrect answer, and this continued down the line to the real test subject who, against his will, gave the same incorrect answer. What the real test subject didn't know was that the other subjects were actors--they were answering the questions wrong on purpose, meanwhile the real subject knew the correct answers but still chose to answer incorrectly.

The human psyche has a predisposition to conformity. Just like the real test subject, we all receive feelings of pressure, like anxiety, fear of disapproval, and self-consciousness--feelings that make us want to conform and give up our values. The real test subject knew the correct answers but went with the group so they wouldn't be unique.

As a child, I was very impressionable. I looked up to my brother and I wanted to be like him. So I dressed like him and acted like him. Little did I know that I was conforming to whatever ideals my brother had without discovering my own. When I started discovering myself, I stopped conforming. My brother earns a lot of money, but we chose different paths. I developed my own uniqueness by doing things differently than my brother or friends.

Maintaining Your Uniqueness

Conformity is the opposite of uniqueness. If you want to be different, you have to reduce feelings of pressure, be unafraid to showcase your talents, and stay true to your unique self. Tapping into your own uniqueness and doing what is correct to you is more difficult than you think. When you are around others you may feel those feelings of pressure, like fear and anxiety. Those feelings are understandable because there are real consequences to rejecting conformity--you can be ostracized from a group, bullied, and lose social status. But if your friends would ostracize, bully, or think less of you, then they don't care about your uniqueness and shouldn't be your friends anyway. What is the sense of trying to fit in if you lose your own unique identity in the process? Unfortunately, people who lose their identity often fall victim to mental disorders—depression being one of them; that price is too high and it's definitely not worth it. Practice being different. In order to stand out, you have to embody the opposite of those feelings of pressure—

when you feel anxious, relax; fear, be bold; and self-consciousness, be comfortable in your own skin. Then you can allow your uniqueness to shine.

Anxiety and Pressure

Anxiety is what you feel when you are unsure of the outcome and you can't control it. When people get anxious, they end up making bad decisions.

Pressure, such as peer pressure, is one of the more common reasons we conform; interestingly, it doesn't have to be pressure by persuasion or intimidation, it can be pressure by influence, advertisements, media, or our own perceptions of self. Maybe you have seen lots of advertisements promoting someone's ideal beauty, success, happiness, lifestyle, family, etc. At times it may make you feel insecure and inadequate, but don't be pressured by that stuff. First, most of them are lies. Second, remember that those things are the perceptions of other people. You have your own mind and ideas, and you should embrace them. If people try pressuring you to conform, tell them exactly what you think, tell them you're not interested, you've got your own plans and ideas.

Being different is strength. Any great person you can think of is different. Do not give in to the pressure. Be unique. Be different. Besides, there is something innately boring and superficial about people who look and act the same.

Fear

Fear is not the same as anxiety. Where anxiety is a response to perceived danger, fear is a response to actual danger. Our human race can go extinct quickly if we don't have fear; it is what triggers our fight or flight response. However, fear is also used as a tool to keep us oppressed and sedated. When we allow fear to control our movements, when we get afraid of being ourselves because our teachers will look down on us, or a bully will keep picking on us, or some terrorist will try to hurt us, then we are not being unique, but controlled. In order to be great, we have to break out of fear and all other forms of subjugation. The next time you get fearful of something or someone, remember that there are more people out there who are fearful of the same things, and if you want to be great, then you'll have to take the first step toward building up your courage and confronting your fears. When you do these things, you are automatically being different than those who live with fear.

Get rid of feelings of pressure by confronting your fears, anxieties, and insecurities; but most importantly, be **d**ifferent.

4. Design

*If you don't design your own life plan, chances are you'll fall into
someone else's plan. And guess what they have planned for you?
Not much.* - Jim Rohn

Observe where you are now—in your room, in a car, in a

building, on a bus, at a park. Observe the details that give your

location its appearance, feel, and functionality. Acknowledge that

the look, feel, and function of the place is a blueprint; it has a

design and a designer. In this life, you are your own designer.

Once you understand this, you will understand the need for a

design—blueprint, plan, strategy—for your life.

As a child, triggers from your parents, friends, family, and

environment play a large role in your design. Your mind is so

impressionable and inexperienced as a child that the things you

see, hear, taste, and touch add to your molding. Throughout your

life, you make decisions, such as whether to listen to your parents,

do your chores, finish your homework, lie, go out with your friends

or not, etc. The decisions you make in response to the triggers around you are synonymous with drawing a picture on a canvas—you draw yourself into the person you are now.

You are (and always have been) a product of a design. But what you probably don't realize is that you are the designer. You make decisions every day in reaction to the triggers around you. So you always are the designer of your life because every action and reaction is a stroke of a paintbrush that will eventually lead to a permanent drawing. Now is the time to either continue improving this design, update it, refurbish it, or get an entirely new one.

Plan

A design exercise that usually produces good results is the five year plan. The five year plan is when you write out what you want to accomplish for each upcoming year. The biggest problem with the five year plans I see is that most people write them down, get excited about them, but forget them later on, which results in a failure to execute the plan.

Here are 7 tips for making a powerful five year plan. Write down each of the five years. Make the plan long enough to warrant transformation in the future but short enough to hold yourself accountable for it sooner than later. Your plan should be so detailed that it is the blueprint of the vision you dreamed about in the previous chapter. Depending on what you want to accomplish, your plan should be flexible where it needs to be, but mainly strict. It should be measurable, so you can tell when you are making progress. You should predict challenges and resources. And you must constantly update the plan.

- Separate the years.

- Make it time bound.

- Make it detailed.

- Make it flexible where it needs to be, but mainly strict.

- Make sure your goals are measurable and achievable.

- Predict challenges and resources.

- Constantly update.

A study conducted by Dominican University of California psychology professor Dr. Gail Matthews showed that people who wrote down their goals, shared the information with a friend, and sent weekly updates to that friend were 33% more successful in accomplishing their stated goals than those who merely formulated goals.[3]

The applicants were sectioned off into 5 groups; as the group number advanced, the responsibilities advanced.

• Group 1 was asked to think about the business-related goals they hoped to accomplish within a four-week block and to rate each goal according to difficulty, importance, the extent to which they had the skills and resources to accomplish the goal, their commitment and motivation, and whether they had pursued the goal before.

• Groups 2-5 were asked to write their goals down, instead of just thinking about the goals, and then rate the goals with the same factors as Group 1.

---

[3] Mathews , Gail. *Goals Research*. Dominican University of California, 2007.

•   Group 3 did all the above and wrote action commitments

for each goal.

•   Group 4 did all the above and shared these commitments

with a friend.

•   Group 5 went the farthest by doing all the above plus

sending a weekly progress report to a friend.

With about seventy six percent of their goals accomplished,

Group 5 was the most successful group out of the other groups at

the end of the experiment. That was no coincidence. The

members of Group 5 designed their lives better. They wrote down

their goals, shared them with friends, and kept themselves

accountable for their goals by sending weekly progress reports. I

want you to put yourself in Group 5.

It is hard to find a successful person who has not created a

design for his/her goals. Some write their goals out, others

envision their goals in detail, while many draw their goals or

surround themselves with pictures of the goals. Jim Carrey wrote a

check for the amount of money he wanted to make, and he

eventually received the check he wanted. Different people create different designs for their lives, what's yours?

As the designer of your life, you have the opportunity to be an artist, even if you think you have no artistic talent. When it comes to your life, you are the artist, the engineer, the sculptor, and the architect.

Bodybuilding is a sport that incorporates fitness, dieting, conditioning, and most importantly, aesthetics. Bodybuilders transform themselves into the physical embodiments of several designs. Ancient greek sculptures designed and sculpted the physiques of men and women, and in bodybuilding, these men and women are doing the same thing by sculpting their bodies into their own designs. In order to achieve their goals, they write down their routines, they keep track of their dieting, and they consistently work out their muscles to achieve their desired physiques. Why can't we apply this level of commitment to our life goals?

Famed bodybuilding champion, actor, governor, and master of design, Arnold Schwarzenegger[4] designed his life as a bodybuilder would design their body for competitions. He jotted down his goals on index cards, which he frequently revised. He kept images of the design he wanted in his room. He broke everything down to repetitions (reps); the more he trained his body and mind through an increased number of reps, the more his results improved. If he was scheduled to deliver a speech, he would do 55 practice reps, as in practice 55 times, and he'd see results in memorization, just as 55 reps of barbell lifting would result in muscle growth. By creating a design before executing, he was able to succeed in bodybuilding, acting, and later, becoming a governor.

Let's say you discover that fitness is a big part of your life, and you dream of having a certain weight. There is a process that is going to get you from the weight you are now to the weight you want; that process begins with a design. It's your job to research

---

[4] Schwarzenegger, Arnold. Total Recall : My Unbelievably True Life Story. New York :Simon & Schuster, 2012. Print.

and create correct meal plan and exercise routine needed to reach your goal.

Design is important because it gives structure to dreams. There are many people out there who **d**ream but don't act on their dreams because they don't know how. There are also people who dream and go straight to action, but they skip the design step which makes their actions ineffective. If two nations are at war, and one nation has a strategy, but the other does not, the nation with the strategy is more likely to win.

Imagine wanting to lose 50 pounds, but not having a design for it. Without a design, you can end up throwing yourself into the fire by doing any weight loss program out there that promises quick results. You can end up losing more than 50 pounds, like 100 pounds, due to malnourishment, and then your life will be defined by yo-yo dieting. Why put yourself through that trouble?

You don't have time to waste; you want to make your mark on this earth, and it's important that you do so effectively, or else you will lose time going back and forth, up and down, and around and around, like a yo-yo. Create a design for how you will execute

your dream!

5. Detail

The difference between something good and something great is

attention to detail. - Charles R. Swindol

Consider the study by Dr. Gail Matthews in the last chapter. The

5th group was the most successful because their plan was more

accountable, written out, and *detailed.*

The next time you decide to skip through a product's terms

and conditions, think about how a company can legally infringe on

your rights, take extra money from you without your knowledge,

and even, relinquish itself from any responsibilities. Reading

through the fine print may be annoying or time consuming at first,

but it is necessary if you want to protect yourself as a consumer,

employee, or business owner. Being secure enhances quality of

life because you have one less thing to stress over; so

understanding the details along your path to success will help you

identify and avoid potential harms, which will increase your

security, and in effect, improve your quality of life.

Furthermore, think about the opportunity you flunked because you couldn't specify your good traits, or think about the class or sport you dropped out of because you didn't work on your weaknesses enough. Working on the details secures your position as one of the top picks for an opportunity, it assures that you can smoothly carry out a task, it saves you from giving up, and it stops you from doubting yourself.

Detail is all around you; it is the difference between shooting a ball that bounces off of a hoop or one that goes in, it's the difference between landing the job that pays well or settling, it's the difference between making a lasting first impression or not.

Maybe you are a really good hitter on the football field, but your agility needs to improve. Working on your speed and balance will improve your agility, which will assure that you are irreplaceable on the field. Understanding what you need to work on is synonymous with understanding the details.

Name one small goal in your life, such as saving money or having enough time to spend with your family, and I guarantee that if you pay more attention to the details, you can reach that goal. You can reach it because you can pinpoint the problem that blocks you, then you can work on it.

I believe one percent of the human population actually pays attention to detail, and that is usually a result of failures and past experiences. When you learn to ride a bike, you fall down numerous times. Learning to ride a bike the correct way comes from a detailed process of falling, getting back up, and keeping your balance. Your mind and body have to subconsciously learn the details the more you practice—soon your mind is telling you where to put your hands and how to shift your weight. The more you practice, the more instinctual your actions become. Then, if you want to be even more detailed, to the level of the one percent, you will practice fanciful tricks, like popping wheelies.

In order to be a part of the one percent that pays attention to detail, you have to pinpoint the problem and practice fixing that problem until it's no longer a problem. However, understand that working on the details takes time; if you are in a rush, if you rather generalize, if you want a sensational life, then details are not for you, and neither is success.

Detail in All Fields

In the world of sales, detail is what gets the client's attention. In the world of art, detail differentiates a superb piece from a mediocre one; in teaching, detail allows the teacher's message to resonate with the student; in the world of business, detail helps companies stay afloat instead of going bankrupt; in the world of stocks, detail makes an investor stay in or get out at the correct time; in the world of music, detail changes the mood of the listener.

Musicians are usually very detailed—no matter what genre. A lot of times, musicians **d**evelop a sixth sense for sound, some of them even develop perfect pitch where they can name the keys that are played at any given time. A unique example of detail was in 1978 at the Peace Concert where Bob Marley, one of many performers, played his greatest hits at the National Stadium in Kingston, Jamaica. A lot of people consider this a highlight of peaceful relations in Jamaica when Bob Marley brought Michael

Manley and Edward Seaga—political rivals vying for the Prime

Minister position in the 1980 election in Jamaica—up to the stage

to shake hands.

During all the commotion and passion in the crowd, no one

really noticed that Marley's band made a misstep. Marley was in a

state of euphoria as he improvised the words for his One Love

song. But when a band member used the wrong key, Marley

grabbed the mic and said, "ya better watch watch, watch what ya

doin."   Everyone thought this was just a part of his improvisation

act, but it wasn't. He used this command as a double entendre to

warn the band to get back on key, while also warning the "powers

that be" to watch out. The audience didn't notice the details.

Truthfully, only a person who is trained in musical notes, or

someone who expected this reaction, would have caught the

misstep. Often in life, we don't catch the details because we are

not well trained to catch them.

Fresh out of college, I went for my first interview for the job I really wanted. Thinking I was an indispensable applicant because of my degree, I didn't practice interview questions and answers much. In fact, during the interview, I thought I did well. I later learned that I flopped because I lacked detail in my application and interview. I failed to practice detailed responses to interview questions, and I didn't fully explain my good qualities. The interviewer told me that his company received a lot of applicants, but detail is what distinguishes a good application from a great one, and they would rather select the great ones. I learned the hard way that more opportunities open up to you when you are detailed.

You cannot honestly have details without a **d**esign first. That's like trying to build the Barclay's Stadium in Brooklyn, New York, without any blueprints. Consider the design of the human body; you'd start off with a skeleton, then you'd add the details, like the nervous system, the heart, the blood vessels, the muscles, the tendons, the organs, and the list goes on. The details make the human body function.

Detail is in every part of our lives, but we take detail for granted. We come home to a house that is designed by an architect with detail and precision, however we don't always care for the texture and material of the house and rooms. We care more about using the house for shelter and comfort. The same can be said of our cars; they take us from our houses to our doctors' offices, from the offices to our jobs, from our jobs to markets, and from parks to restaurants. We are able to make our cars reverse, accelerate and break, but we don't have to see the functionality inside of them; we don't have to see the gas fueling the engine, or the cylinders moving, or the brakes stopping the wheels. As long as when we press the acceleration and turn the steering wheel, the car follows our command, but the details make the car move.

People who specialize in a field know the details of that field. For instance, a mechanic's mind is filled with the intricacies of the various parts that make a car function properly. Their senses are in tune with that car; that goes for anyone who is a master at a craft, they see the profession in more than a singular dimension, but in three dimensions. Consider how a good CEO can see the connections between employees, paychecks, return on investment (ROI), departments, investors, lenders, and so on.

As a stockbroker, I had to pay attention to the details of my potential clients. I had to find ways to build rapport with them; if they had a family, then I would share relatable stories, if they had a specific problem, I would hone in on that problem and explain how I could help.

Maybe you don't have all the details of your **d**esign yet, but you do have the ability to research. You have the means to research the details of your goal and to understand it thoroughly with books, online resources, and personal stories. After you create your design, use the tools at your disposal to make your design more detailed.

Abraham Lincoln famously said, "if you give me six hours to cut down a tree, I'll spend the first four hours sharpening the axe." So if you have six months to do a task, four months should

be spent creating a design, ironing out the details and gathering the

proper expertise.

6. Direction

If one advances confidently in the direction of his dreams, and endeavors to live the life which he has imagined, he will meet with a success unexpected in common hours. - Henry David Thoreau

Imagine an immense ship with clean sails, an intricate design, an intelligent captain, and cutting edge technology. The captain of the ship and his crew are preparing to sail from Europe to Asia—it's actually a dream of his. He has a detailed plan for how he is going to get there. He declares it to everyone who listens. He has a specific day for when he is going to sail, then he sails out for ten months. Finally, when he lands with his ship and crew, he realizes that he didn't land in Asia, but in the Americas.

If you're Christopher Columbus, then this misdirection might have been helpful for your career, but in the off-chance that you are not, having the right direction is your best bet. Direction is immensely important in goal setting because it is how you get from one part of your life to the next. Not having a direction can leave you lost for days, weeks, years, and an entire lifetime. So ask yourself, "am I following the right direction?"

Go back to your childhood, and imagine waking up on one hot, simmering day at your friend's house. Along with the other cool thoughts that cross your mind, you think of ice-cream. As time goes by, you **d**evelop a craving for ice-cream. You ask your friend for the closest ice-cream shop in the area; he tells you there's a nice one on a block called Front street. Then you create a **d**esign, a plan, for how to get there; you'll drive your car or borrow your friend's bike and get directions from your friend. Now you know where to go and how to get there, so you leave. You are **d**etermined to get that ice-cream. While you ride, there are no accidents and no problems, nothing is in your way. You reach the address on Front street, exactly where your friend told you to go, but there are no ice-cream shops. Well, this must be some sort of mistake.

If you planned correctly and you have no problem followed your friend's precise directions, then why are you at the wrong place?

In truth, that ice-cream shop was about two blocks away from where you ended up. You followed the directions your friend gave you, but something went wrong. Either you interpreted the directions wrong, or your friend made a mistake. Nonetheless, there was miscommunication somewhere and you ended up lost along that path.

Miscommunication

This analogy is synonymous with the many plans, professions, hobbies, and activities in our daily lives. We can be extremely skilled, have many plans, focus really hard, and have good attributes, but we find ourselves in destinations that aren't where we want to be. A company may have a great CEO, good workers, and an awesome product, but bad return on investment. Why is that? The company is going in the wrong direction—there is a big miscommunication between the CEO and his workers or bosses, so the leadership needs to change.

Some people forget this but Apple was a small company compared to the global, multibillion-dollar company it is now.

However, it was always very innovative back in the 1970's and 80's. What brought Apple into the 21st century was a change in direction. When Steve Jobs left Apple in 1985, the company soon ran into debt and sales problems. Jobs was asked to come back as a fill-in CEO for the company in 1997 to help get the company back on track. Jobs changed the direction of the company by changing the marketing scheme; he changed the way Apple targeted customers and who they targeted; he presented Apple as the new, hip, personal computer that would defeat the big boys in the industry, like IBM. Soon after the company changed its direction, it started doing well. When the iPod came out, it was a revolutionary product. But what really made Apple huge, was the touchscreen iPhone, a device that was like no other cellphone.

In life, there aren't many things worse than working really hard toward a specific goal but later learning that you are going the wrong way. Consider a James "Whitey" Bulger. He is a man who represents leadership, strong mental stability, health, wit, skill, intelligence, and risk taking—he had all of these wonderful attributes, but he chose the path of the criminal. He was on the FBI's most wanted list for twelve years because of a crime syndicate he started in South Boston in the 1970s.

Right after Bulger was captured in 2011, three high school girls decided to ask him about his experience with leadership for their high school leadership project.[5] As awkward as that may seem, these girls wanted to try a different angle from the usual dead presidents approach. They figured he possessed leadership qualities, albeit in the criminal underworld. Surprisingly, he wrote back from a federal penitentiary in Sumterville, FL. He said, "My life was wasted and spent foolishly, brought shame and suffering on my parents and siblings and will end soon." He continued, "Advice is a cheap commodity some seek it from me about crime — I know only one thing for sure — If you want to make crime pay — 'Go to Law School.'"

---

[5] Ryan, David L. "'My Life Was Wasted,' James 'Whitey' Bulger Says in Letter to Students - The Boston Globe." BostonGlobe.com, The Boston Globe, 27 June 2015, www.bostonglobe.com/metro/2015/06/27/whitey-bulger-letter-life-was-wasted/ irYL38W7IxI5ycoEpDohkI/story.html.

He advised the girls not to focus on him, but to think about law school if they are interested in being leaders on criminal issues. He also noted in the letter that he "took the wrong road," but his brother, William Bulger, former President of both the Massachusetts Senate and the University of Massachusetts, was "A Better Man than I."

The story of James "Whitey" Bulger and his brother, William "Billy" Bulger, is an astonishing example of how people with similar qualities can go in opposite directions. They both had leadership potential, but one chose a fruitful direction meanwhile the other chose a fruitless one.

You can have some of the greatest attributes known to man, yet if you spend your time being unproductive, abusing drugs and substances, being idle, ignoring the correct outlet for your talents, distracting yourself, and spending time with negative people, then you are likely to end up in the wrong place —in the case of James "Whitey" Bulger, it was two life sentences.

Direction is the difference between a man who observes a few trees and a man who observes the entire forest. It's the difference between a woman who is on board a ship and a woman who navigates the ship. It's the difference between one who is the leader of a criminal enterprise and one who is the leader of a legal multibillion-dollar company.

To have the right direction, you need to **d**eclare your **d**ream, have a detailed design, and match those with detailed research on "how" you can reach your dream.

Maybe your goal is to fight crime. One direction is law school. But even further, you want to research the kinds of law schools that match your qualities because that will determine the kind of lawyer you become and your experiences immediately after law school. You can be a law grad with no debt and a job lined up, or a law grad with tons of debt opportunities.

The choices you make matter most in directing your life. When you are in college, work experiences, internships, classes, and organizations all matter—they are self-directing activities. These activities shape your experience and shape you as a person.

Be self-directed—choose how you spend your time, choose who you spend it with, choose what information you listen to, even choose the books you read. Don't get me wrong, randomly reading something isn't bad, but self-directed people usually *choose* to read random books. Direction boils down to a **d**ecision, and these choices direct us to who we will become.

For all you know, you can be the one who gets lost looking for that ice-cream shop, runs into a stranger, politely talks to that stranger, and that stranger directs you on the correct path. This is just like any other activity in life. You may get thrown off of your path, but the next few choices you make will help you get right back on track.

7. Decision

In any moment of decision, the best thing you can do is the right thing, the next best thing is the wrong thing, and the worst thing you can do is nothing. - Theodore Roosevelt

This journey to greatness is a fragile one, the wrong decision can point you in the wrong **d**irection; though you can always change your direction, it can take a too long and you don't have time to waste.

In order to make decisions that are going to put you in the right direction, first you should understand the nature of a decision. According to Webster's Dictionary, a decision is a conclusion you reach after deliberation and consideration. So if you do something out of instinct or impulse, you are not making a decision at all; but if you think before you act, you are making a decision. This is one characteristic about humans that set us apart from animals--we make decisions, while animals act on instinct. This is not to say that all of our instincts are bad; our instincts help us survive, but simply put, instincts alone will not help you thrive and become

great.

Why are Decisions Important?

The decisions you make are the most important parts of your life.

If I had to **d**efine a life, it would be an accumulation of decisions.

In the *7 Habits of Highly Effective People*, author Stephen Covey

talks about a World War II Holocaust survivor named Viktor Frankl

who breaks down the importance of decision making and power.[6]

Frankl is attributed with saying, "Between stimulus and response,

there is a space. In that space is our power to choose our response.

In our response lies our growth and our freedom."

This quote is one of my favorites. Imagine that no matter

where you end up in life, you can always rely on your decisions for

empowerment. Frankl was humiliated, torn from his family, and

denigrated in Nazi death camps, yet he found power in the way he

---

[6] Covey, Stephen R. *The 7 Habits of Highly Effective People.* Franklin Covey, 1998.

responded to the terrible stimuli around him. He was able to free

his mind and keep it intact.

Decision Making Mentality

This mentality is what you need to have—the mentality of taking

responsibility for yourself and actions while finding strength in the

decisions you make. Think of life as a journey through a jungle.

As you are trekking through that jungle, you'll need to make good

decisions in order to stay on a successful path or get back on track

if you fall off.

If you fall into quicksand, you must make the correct

decisions to get yourself out; you might have to crawl onto the

most sturdy surface, find a vine that you can use as a rope, or call

for help; these are all actions which you must decide to make.

What you should avoid is acting on impulse where you start

panicking. Quicksand, like most problems, is exacerbated by our

lack of knowledge. The truth is that you will not drown from

quicksand, just as you will not be permanently hurt from the

temporary troubles you go through in life. Start making decisions that you are responsible for instead of impulse actions that you make excuses for, and you'll exercise your brain to make better decisions while under pressure. Just as weights build the body's muscles, responsibility builds the brain's muscles. You'll make some bad decisions along your journey, but you'll learn from them, and next time, you'll better prepare yourself.

You will always be in this jungle of life, and there will come a time when you reach the top of a cliff and you have the decision to jump into a body of water; that's a decision with consequences, for which you have to be responsible. In life, you shouldn't allow yourself to be peer pressured into doing things you would normally disregard, but you definitely have to take some risks in order to reach your goals. So maybe jumping off of that cliff is the risk you need to take, but just because you have to take risks doesn't mean you should do so blindly; you should prepare yourself for the potential consequences of those risks. Too many people have broken their backs jumping off of cliffs, literally.

How Do We Master Our Decisions

If you want to make better decisions, you have to examine the factors involved and evaluate the harms and benefits.

In order to mitigate the harm of your decisions, examine the factors involved and then evaluate the harms and benefits. Some examples of factors are *you*, your environment, and your relationships. With every potential decision, ask yourself if you're being influenced by the people around you, your environment, or your own values. Factors other than yourself, like your family, friends, and environment can influence you for the better or worse, so going with your own values isn't always the best decision, especially if you are selfish or obnoxious. Once you understand what is influencing you, you can better understand the benefits or consequences of your actions. If you are doing a negative thing because you are in a negative environment and you are being pressured by negative people, then most likely, the outcome will be negative; 1 plus 1 still equals 2. After you understand what's influencing you to make a decision, you must evaluate the benefits and harms of the decision by weighing them. If you have a blank

sheet of paper where you can put both benefits and harms on

separate columns next to each other, and you are able to write

down more benefits than harms for a particular decision, then that

decision will most likely have better outcomes.

First, examine each individual factor, then weigh the harms

and benefits. So if you decide to become a lawyer, why? Is it

something you really like? Or is it something your parents want?

Or is it something you think you should do because your friends

are doing it or the media is telling you it's a good decision?

If you are about to fight someone, why? Did someone peer

pressure you? What do you value? What are the potential harms

and benefits?

Examining the factors and evaluating the harms and

benefits will help you to deeply understand your decisions, so you

can take full responsibility of your actions and not use the excuse

that "I didn't know." Even if you are short on time when you have to make a quick decision, step back, take a deep breath, think the

decision through, then make the decision after some thought.

Assign Value

So you're still trekking through the jungle, and there is the

possibility of jumping off of the cliff. If you want to do that, you

have to measure the factors involved. Why do you want to do it?

If it's because of peer pressure, then that's a terrible reason and the

consequence is potential self-harm without impressing your

friends. Can you swim? If the answer is no, then the consequence

is you could drown. Is the jump very far up? If so, then the

consequence is you can potentially break your back when you hit

the water. Is it dangerous? Maybe there are rocks at the bottom of

the waterfall. If so, then you could critically or fatally hurt

yourself. What's in the water? If there are exotic animals that you

are not familiar with, then you should find out which animals are

there. Understand that fear is not a factor here, you want to be

fearless in your decisions but not stupid.

Once you've examined the various factors involved, and you've weighed the harms and benefits, assign values to those harms and benefits. What do you value the most? Being safe and doing what's in your ability or jumping to impress others? If it's really important to you, then after examining the factors, do you still want to do it? If you do, be fearless in your decision and do it. Risks are meant to be taken in order to get ahead, but once you make a decision, go all the way.

It is widely believed that we are solely products of our environment, but that idea ignores our human will, ingenuity, creativity and innovation. We can be influenced by the environment and triggers around us, but if we are solely products of that environment, we would never have developed much from 100,000 years ago to the 21st century. In fact, we would still be living in caves because we wouldn't have a desire to advance ourselves. But we are constantly shaping our environment, challenging the triggers around us, and gaining power through the decisions we make.

Every decision matters. I believe what Bud Fox said in the movie *Wall Street* is true, "life comes down to a few moments."[7] But what Fox forgot to say was that in-between those few moments, we have to make small decisions that will lead to those few moments where we make big decisions. So making sure that you wake up early in the morning is a small decision but it will lead to huge payoffs. Deciding to be well informed about whatever endeavors you choose, such as an interview, will lower your chances of making a mistake. Deciding to go to work on time every day will lower your chances of being fired, deciding to eat healthy meals every day will lower your risk of getting diabetes or other health problems, deciding to stay away from dysfunctional relationships will help you clear your mind so you can focus on your success and greatness.

Along with the importance of decision making, the responsibility we place on ourselves is important. We get mad at people who disrespect us, but we fail to get mad at ourselves for

[7] Stone, Oliver, director. *Wall Street*. Twentieth Century Fox Film Corporation, 1987.

making friends with these questionable people. No matter how wrong an environment or person is to you, there are always two responsibilities. Sure, the environment and the person who harmed you are at fault, but you are responsible for distancing yourself from that environment and person.

Joining a fraternity for the better making of men, like Alpha Phi Alpha Fraternity, Inc., was a huge decision for me. I had what is known as a "hood" mentality while growing up—I emotionally and immaturely reacted to people who I thought wronged me. Often I'd react with slurs, threats, or violence. So naturally, I got into a lot of fights and trouble. When the opportunity came for me to join a group of professionally like-minded individuals, I examined the factors involved. I asked myself, what is influencing me to make this decision? The truth was that I wanted to change my life for the better. Then I weighed the benefits and harms. The benefits definitely outweighed any potential harms. Trust me, this book would never have been written if I didn't make that life changing decision.

Think about your decisions before you act, examine the

factors involved, evaluate the harms and benefits, and assign value.

8. Declare

I declare to you that woman must not depend upon the protection of man, but must be taught to protect herself, and there I take my stand. - Susan B. Anthony

It isn't enough to discover, dream, design, and decide; but you must declare your dreams, declare your goals, and in effect, declare your life. Remember Group 5 from Dr. Mathews' study in chapter 4? They weren't only successful because they created detailed designs for their goals, but they were accountable for their goals— they declared their goals more often than the other participants. They had to tell their goals to a friend and consistently send that friend progress reports. Think about when you tell someone your goal one week, then a month later, you see that person again and they ask you about the goal. How bad do you feel when you have no progress to report?

Declaring your dreams gives those dreams legs. Go back to the founding of America—the founding fathers discovered the potential the colonies had to revolt against King George III, then they dreamed of becoming independent of England, they created a design for this new country, and then they declared it in the Declaration of Independence, the Articles of Confederation and later, the Constitution of The United States of America.

Without these steps, there is no United States. There is no U.S. without the constant reinforcement of that declaration during congressional meetings or during war or in the everyday lives of citizens; in this way, the U.S. has to be accountable for its declaration.

Now in your life, you must create a declaration for yourself. Declare your dreams, plans, and passions to those you trust. Declare your dreams and passions to those who hate you. If someone doubts your capabilities, tell them exactly what you are going to do out loud. Declare your designs to those who believe in you; tell your parents that you will be that lawyer you want to be. If your teachers cast doubt, tell them that you're going to prove them wrong.

The beauty about declaring things is that the declaration is a speech act. Declarations come in the form of promises, pledges, assertions, threats and more. When you declare something, you aren't saying something, but you are *doing* something. Once you've declared it, time opens up a space. Time has recorded your declaration and is awaiting its fulfillment. The people you declare your dream to will always have that declaration in the back of their minds, and your reputation will now depend on the fulfillment of your declaration. You are now tied to your declaration; you can either succeed or fail trying, but defaulting is not an option. If you default on your declarations, you will be labeled a liar who can always lie again.

As a child, I told my mother and father that I'd be successful; I declared it all the time. Now imagine if I defaulted on that declaration; of course my parents would still love me, but that idea I planted in their minds, and in my own mind, would not sprout if I defaulted on my declaration. What if they believed in my dreams and I failed them?

The fate of the defaulter and liar is enough motivation to want success in life. When I declare something, that declaration creeps into my veins, it creeps into my thoughts, actions, and

desires. If I declare something but then default on trying, I become

a liar; lying is that easy. I would never want to be known as a liar;

I take pride in integrity.

Look Like a Butterfly, Sting Like a Bee

Muhammad Ali is a perfect example of a man who declares his

life. From a young age, during an era of suffocating racial

inequality and oppression, Ali, then called Cassius Clay, declared

his greatness. Despite his many setbacks—his grades in school

were consistently bad, he struggled with reading, he barely

graduated from high school in 1960—he still boisterously told

everyone around him that he would be a champion. He later

proved it when he won the light-heavyweight boxing gold medal at

the Athens Olympic Games the same year he barely graduated. Ali

represented more than his circumstance; he was an icon of

defiance who ignited tremendous passion—either you loved him or

you hated him. He was a figure of strength, pride, charm,

charisma, beauty, dissent, and courage that transcended boxing alone. Captivating millions of people, his aura rose to the heights of entertainment, intellectualism, and perseverance as he appeared on numerous late night shows and became the most popular man in America.[8]

Yes, he was hardworking; yes, he developed a lot of skills; yes, he was clever; but the source of his strength could be found in his voice. His voice was one of confidence; he was so confident, that he'd predict, in detail, his victories. In 1963 he said he'd beat Henry Cooper in round 5, and he did! He walked up to that ring with a king's crown declaring that he was the greatest boxer even before the fight started. In fact, he told the entire world that he was the greatest boxer of all time, and whether you believed it or not, he convinced you and himself that he was the greatest boxer of all time.

Before the 1974 Ali and Frazier fight, when Ali was asked what he'd do if Joe Frazier beat him, he answered, "I can't lose. I'm not worried about losing, there's no reason for me to lose." He

---

[8] Myers, Walter Dean. *The Greatest: Muhammad Ali*. Scholastic Inc., 2002.

even joked about leaving the U.S. and going to another country out of embarrassment if he loss. Imagine the shame Ali would have felt after talking all of that junk and claiming that he was the greatest of all time just to have those words equal absolutely nothing. That alone is scary—so it is motivation.

Whenever Ali declared his goals, he gained supporters and haters. The trick was that both groups of people motivated him. You should declare your dreams, and put yourself in a position for both groups to motivate you too.

Supporters believe in your dreams, they keep you going when you get tired, and haters will hope you fail so they can prove that your declaration is impossible. You don't have to declare your goals to the point of bragging—that's what Ali did, and it worked for him. Being humble will certainly get you far in life, but you do have to declare your goals.

Why Declaring is Important

How do you expect to become successful if you don't tell people your goals? Of course you have to pick and choose what you tell and who you tell it to. When you declare your goals to the correct people (friends, family, supportive groups, people in the industry, mentors) you'll have more than just yourself looking out for you. The people you declare your goals to can eventually point you in the right direction, give you the resources you need to become successful, believe in your dreams and support you. Having that supportive community or system behind you can keep you on track when you are less enthused.

When I was in the beginning stages of my business I told it to everyone who I felt was supportive of me. Instead of keeping everything inside, I told my brother, my aunt, and my closest friends. That supportive group kept me going. After I told my aunt about my business goals, she'd ask me about them whenever I saw her during family events. Knowing this was going to be a big talking point for us, I made sure that I had real results every year. I didn't want to see disappointment on her face or mine.

There are only a few people in this world who can stay motivated throughout their entire life. The unexpected parts of life take us off track, but having a supportive group of people around

you will keep you on track by reminding you of your passions, by

supporting your endeavors, and by simply listening to your ideas.

When you declare your goals, you become a mountain

climber who just started climbing the greatest mountain of your

life. Now, you are so far up that you can barely see the ground

below, but you are so far down that you can barely see the tip of

the mountain; nonetheless, you can see that sky. You know that

below are haters, disgraces, despairs, depressions, shames, and if

you are really on that mountain, death. Meanwhile, above you, at

the top of that mountain is glory and fulfillment. You can take

breaks, you can eat, you can sleep, but what you can not do is quit.

You have to keep going up; the risks are too high to go down and

suffer the humiliation. Think of all the people who have high

hopes for you, who love you, who want you to succeed, now think

of their disappointments if you fail.

You can always try something halfway, quit, then tell

people you tried it after the fact, but that is past the stage of accountability—you failed before anyone knew you tried. If you want to go all the way, then you must declare your goals before you've finished pursuing them; you must tell people what you want to do so they can expect it from you, so they can hold you accountable for your words. If you don't declare your goals to gain support and/or hate, then you simply aren't serious about your goals. It's easy to shy away from a path if you haven't declared it as your path A because trying a path does not come with responsibility, but *declaring* a path comes with responsibility. Remember, declarations are not sayings, they are action words.

This is the attitude you must adopt. If your path A isn't working out, then you should redesign your path A, but a path B isn't an option. Now is the time to declare your dream, your path A, and don't quit.

9. Dare

Most people live and die with their music still unplayed. They never dare to try. - Mary Kay Ash

Daring is extremely important because if you dare to be great, if you dare to follow your dreams, if you dare to reach your goals, if you dare to get out of the situation that is holding you back, then you already give yourself a better chance at success than most people in this world; so daring puts you a few steps closer to your goals. It's like that old saying, "if you shoot for the moon but you don't make it, at least you're among those stars."

Daring Against the Odds

It's hard to find someone who doesn't know about Thomas Edison, but it's equally hard to find someone who knows about Nikola Tesla. Both of these larger than life figures embody daredevils.

Thomas Edison dared to build an energy and engineering business in the mid to late 1800's which turned into the General Electric of today. In 1872, after multiple attempts, Edison and his team were able to produce light through electricity in a vacuum tube within an incandescent glass container — also known as the light bulb. He built his business by getting patents for inventions and taking on grand scale projects that would distribute what he produced to the masses.

In the 1880's the main source of electric currency came from Edison's own DC (direct current) motors. The issue with these motors was that the amount of voltage could not be changed once the motor started, and the motor made a dangerous spark which could threaten to cause a fire.

In June of 1884, Tesla, a little known Croatian engineering genius at the time, dared to give up everything he knew to sail to America with only 4 cents in his pockets; he had no job, but a head full of imaginative designs and ways to revolutionize electricity intake with AC (alternate current) motors.[9]

Eventually, Tesla met with Edison, a wealthy inventor and businessman at the time. Edison was interested in Tesla and dared him to improve the way Edison's DC generators functioned.

---

[9] McPherson, Stephanie S. War of the currents : Thomas Edison vs. Nikola Tesla. Minneapolis: Twenty-First Century Books, 2013. Print.

Edison told Tesla that if he was successful, then he'd pay Tesla $50,000, which is about 1 million in today's currency. Tesla accepted the dare and was hired. He then worked from 10:30 a.m. to 5:30 a.m. every day on the generators.

Unfortunately, this dare didn't work well for Tesla because even though he eventually finished the generators, Edison had other ideas. When Tesla went to Edison for payment, Edison laughed at him and said, "You don't understand our American humor." Then Edison offered Tesla a raise, but Tesla was too offended and walked out.

Life after working with Edison was filled with dares—Tesla constantly dared himself to invent new things. Soon, he dared to challenge Edison's DC generators with his own AC generators in the war of the currents of the late 1800s.

After leaving Edison's Electric Light Company, Tesla worked an odd job digging ditches for a year until he couldn't take it anymore. Then he got a few investors to invest in his laboratory. In that lab, he created the AC system that would revolutionize electric power. He received over twenty-two patents for his

system, which soon led to the investment of a wealthy industrialist

named George Westinghouse. Westinghouse offered Tesla about

$1 million for the patents and a stake in his company, which is

worth multi-millions to a billion dollars now. Even though he

agreed to the offer and made a fortune, Tesla's story of daring

didn't end there. He continued to **d**evelop himself. He continued

to **d**are at greater things than his previous accomplishments.

He is the creator of many well known devices, such as the

first known remote controlled device, the first stages of the X-Ray,

the first stages of the radio, hydroelectric power plants,

phosphorescent light bulbs, and the induction motor which powers

numerous devices in the 21st century, like power tools.

Tesla was **d**riven by a **d**esire to improve the living

standards of those around him — instead of being money hungry

like the people he met, he spent all of his money on his life's

passion, and ironically, he died poor but great. This was a man who dared to be **d**ifferent, he dared to follow his **d**reams no matter what the consequences. How daring are you?

"Money does not represent such a value as men have placed on it. All of my money has been invested into experiments with which I have made new discoveries enabling mankind to have a little easier life." - Nikola Tesla

Understanding Dare

Most likely, you have heard the term, "I dare you" before. Either someone challenged you to do something, you were threatened with a potentially negative consequence, or you already did something brash or bold. "I dare you to open the bottle, see what happens to you" sounds different from " I dare you to open the bottle before they come back," and they both sound different from, "How dare you?" One is a threat, the other is a challenge, and the last is a cry of shock for your brashness; however, they all relate to each other. In those three examples either you were being given the opportunity to act bold or you already did.

To dare implies that you understand the consequences of your actions, it also implies that what you dare to **do** is possible. Jumping off of a seven story building and expecting to be "ok" is not a dare, it's an attempted suicide; the probability that you will survive or live form that jump without any lifelong damage is very low.

The sort of dares you should search for in life are the ones that will make you great.

I dared a lot in my life. I dared to leave a well paying job in order to start my own ambulette business. When my family and friends found out, they thought I was nuts. In 2012 the stock market was hitting new highs every day, so I was making a ton of money. As a good partner should, my wife questioned my **decision** to leave that business. She said, "so this is what you're going to **do**? You are done with stocks?" But when she knew I was serious and passionate about it, she was happy for me. Sure I started off slow, and I didn't have the same amount of money I did as a stockbroker, but as the years went by, my business grew to where I was just as comfortable as I was as a stockbroker. I took a chance

on my dreams; I left everything behind and believed in myself.

Even if it didn't work out, at least I dared to be great. Will you

dare to be great?

10. Deliberate

I am deliberate and afraid of nothing. - Audre Lorde

In this book, I teach you the traits you need to achieve greatness and success. These are traits that separate a Kobe Bryant from a basketball player, or a Warren Buffet from a bad investor.

Luck

If you think luck is the reason for the success of people like Kobe Bryant and Warren Buffet, let me help you rethink your understanding of success. There is no luck and no privilege that will keep you from a loss. Gravity is the natural law of earth. What goes up, comes down. Humans begin as the inferior species, we begin at a low level—in fact, all organisms begin at a low level. There is only a **one to two percent** difference between the human and the chimpanzee.[10] That one to two percent is where we get all the depths of human civilization, such as cultures, arts, humanities,

---

[10]"DNA: Comparing Humans and Chimps." *AMNH*, www.amnh.org/exhibitions/permanent-exhibitions/human-origins-and-cultural-halls/anne-and-bernard-spitzer-hall-of-human-origins/understanding-our-past/dna-comparing-humans-and-chimps/. Accessed 25 Sept. 2017.

sciences, mathematics, quantum physics, and more; yet when we think of a chimpanzee, we don't think of a species that is similar to us. Weird right?

Becoming Deliberate

So humans are about 99 percent similar to chimpanzees, but in our understanding of what it means to be human, we consider being similar to a chimpanzee a low standing. Then how do we advance ourselves to become hunters and gatherers from that low standing? Here are the 4 Cs of our advancement:

1. Concentrate on our problems and solutions.

2. Communicate our problems and solutions to others.

3. Create tools.

4. Contribute to these tools.

Concentrating, communicating, creating, and contribution are not lucky traits, they are *deliberate*. Imagine yourself 70,000 years ago; food is scarce, there is no such thing as money, there is no market, there is you and your social group versus the dangers of earth-ravishing storms, wild and strong beasts, and crippling starvation. If your mind is constantly racing, if you are constantly distracted like a chimpanzee, then it is hard to understand big concepts. In order to **d**eal with your immediate problems, you must allow your mind to focus on these problems. You start thinking about the different ways to solve your problems. This concentration process also leads to better communication with your tribe because you can **d**iscover solutions to overcome communication barriers. Through a process of trial and error, you begin creating things, such as spears, that will help you solve the problem of catching an animal for food. Not everyone can create, but everyone can certainly contribute their ideas and experiences to make your creation stronger and better.

Although there are other processes that shape the human experience, this general process of concentration, communication, creating, and contributing is what helps human beings advance above other species.

Giant's Shoulders

The 4 Cs is a well known trope of human knowledge, articulated by John of Salisbury, the 12th century writer, and Isaac Newton, the 17th century scientist:

> We are like dwarfs sitting on the shoulders of giants. We see more—and things that are more distant—than they did, not because our sight is superior or because we are taller than they, but because they raise us up, and by their great stature add to ours.[11]

Understand that where you work, where you live, even some places you visit are the products of ideas concentrated on, created, communicated, and contributed to for years; this is an ongoing cycle. Facebook, for example, is not possible without the internet or the websites and social mechanisms created over the last twenty years. It was an idea that went through a process of concentration, creation, and communication; thanks to the contribution of billions of people, it is now successful. The same

---

[11] Newton, Isaac. "Letter from Sir Isaac Newton to Robert Hooke". *Historical Society of Pennsylvania*. Retrieved 7 August 2016.

concept can be applied to all fields. The government is a product

of the concentration, creation, and communication of laws to the

public that are contributed to by the citizens and lawmakers;

literature is no different in that respect—there is no Toni Morrison

without James Baldwin, William Faulkner, and Zora Neal Hurston;

finance—the stock market didn't create itself; education—

institutions must continuously figure out ways to help their

students prosper; politics—society has come a long way from the

days of kings and queens. You will see the cycle of the 4 Cs in any

field you come across. But what's the common root in this cycle?

Deliberation.

What I'm telling you is, we humans are able to advance

ourselves one percent from a chimpanzee by being deliberate. We

deliberately concentrate on our problems in order to create

solutions. We deliberately concentrate on our wants and needs in

order to achieve them. If humans are able to advance ourselves

one percent from a chimpanzee by deliberately concentrating,

communicating, creating, and contributing, then why can't we deliberately concentrate, communicate, create, and contribute in order to become .0001% better than we are at this moment? Why can't you intentionally concentrate on being .0001% better than you are now? If a one percent difference is an enormous difference in intellect, such as the difference between a human and a chimpanzee, then there is a .0001% difference between me—a terrible basketball player—and Kobe Bryant, one of the greatest basketball players in the world.

If you want to be better than you are now, if you want to go from what you are now to Kobe Bryant's level, then you have to be deliberate. When he was young, Kobe's main problem was his shot; so he concentrated on shooting, and created a plan. That is being deliberate! He woke up every day at 5 am to practice his shot, and he would shoot from different parts of the court over four hundred times. That is deep concentration, that is how one solves a problem.

By concentrating on his skills, he created a name for himself; he communicated to the world, through his skills and voice, that he was one of the most passionate, hardworking, and skillful players ever to play the sport. Finally, he contributed to the sport by showing younger generations how to elevate their game.

Being down is easy, losing is easy, being unskilled is easy. That's where we start as humans. But we've advanced thanks to our deliberate process of concentration, communication, creation, and contribution. Luck is not a trait of the human being, but deliberation is.

Deliberate thoughts lead to deliberate actions.

When you sit down and think about how you are going to solve a problem, the next step is to test out your thoughts with action—by doing. Now both your thoughts and your actions are deliberate.

11. Do

The way to get started is to quit talking and begin doing. - Walt Disney

What is the sense of having detailed plans, a dream, the correct direction, but no action? So many people push their dreams aside due to a lack of will and understanding. They think if they have more knowledge via books and information, they'll be ready to pursue their dreams. There is a lot of truth to the need for more knowledge, especially when you are in the design stage. You need to get as much knowledge as you possibly can in order to produce optimum results, but you'll never have enough knowledge until you put your skin in the game—until you act. Mistakes are bound to happen, failure is imminent, you have to embrace it and move on. The act of doing is where the learning becomes productive.

As a baby, you learn about your environment from your senses, stimuli, and experiments. Experience and knowledge come into play after you've sensed the environment around you, reacted to the triggers, and experimented with that environment. This is why children play with everything they can get their hands on and put inedible things in their mouths. As a child, you learn language by listening to it, being immersed in it, reacting to it, and experimenting with the words in order to get what you **d**esire, then you start reading to improve your comprehension and communication skills, then you talk more, then you experience more, then you read more, then you talk more, and eventually your language and understanding grows. This cycle of growth begins with having skin in the game. As a baby, you have no choice but to learn about the environment around you—you have no choice but to *do*; so whatever you want to accomplish in life, understand that until you put skin in the game—until you commit to action and make yourself vulnerable, you will gain no real knowledge or experience, and you certainly won't obtain your dreams.

If you have a **d**ream, a **d**esire, something you want to do, then you need to **DO** now and **DO** every day; do when you are feeling down, do when you are feeling happy, do at all times.

How lucky some of us are, to be given a silver spoon and we don't know it. We get to contemplate what we want to accomplish in life, and yet there are people out there who don't have this luxury, people who have to survive on one meal a day, and who can barely go to school because survival is their primary objective—but don't pity them, because they learn to *do* from a young age. Some good examples include people like John Paul Dejoria, Howard Schultz, Do Won Chang, Charlie Chapman, Jim Carrey, J.K. Rowling, and Oprah Winfrey. These people serve as good examples because they come from nothing, their first inclinations are survival. They move up because they already know the bottom, and they will *do* what it takes to never be at the bottom again. So in order to climb that ladder, they *do* every day.

The Formula

Take Harold Simmons for example; here's a man who grew up in a shack without plumbing or electricity, yet he managed to get accepted to the University of Texas where he earned a Bachelor's and a Master's degree in Economics. He got his first big break when he bought a chain of drug stores, and then sold it for $50 million.[12]

George Soros is another example. As a young boy, he survived the Nazi occupation of Hungary, went on to study in London, and later became a billionaire investor.[13] Soros wouldn't have gotten where he did by complaining, looking for an easy way out, or wasting his time. Nor would he have gotten there by being coddled throughout his life; he became successful because he wanted to survive and his dreams mattered more to him than failure. After you understand what it means to survive, then you can transfer the instinct for survival into the instinct for thriving, so you'll be surviving and thriving. The formula for surviving is simple: "if I don't do A then I won't get B".

As plain as the formula is, a lot of us sit back and think that things are going to be handed to us. This belief blurs our vision of

[12] Nance, John J. *Golden Boy: the Harold Simmons Story*. Eakin Press, 2004.

[13] http://www.businessinsider.com/george-soros-billionaire-investor-profile-2017-1

what the results of our actions can be; it blurs our vision of the bottom—a place we can end up 30 years from now.

If you want a clear vision, you should know what the bottom looks like, and what you want the next 30 years of your life to look like. You must understand that though this is where you are now, it is not where you are going to be later. The people who understand this have a clear vision.

This formula is rooted in practicality. It begins with knowing that one action causes another; you need nutritionally dense food and shelter to have a healthy life, so learning how to cook healthy food is a step toward a healthy nutrition, and having a roof over your head will provide protection and comfort. Then there is the need to earn funds for your food and shelter; in order to do that, you need to work. If you are going to work for a living, then you probably want work you enjoy, and that's where an educational training process comes into play. If you want to achieve more, then you will work harder, take on more responsibility, earn more credentials and/or gain more training and

education. When you choose to raise a family, you will adjust
yourself to meet the needs of that family. Understanding the basic
survival process is instinctual, and when someone practically
works to survive, their eyes metaphorically get clearer because
they start to understand the pattern of consequences better than
others; they understand that if A doesn't happen, then B won't
happen.

Blurry vs. Clear Vision

One of the biggest flaws of blurry vision is it stops you from
acting. Think about when you literally have blurry vision. Besides
it being hard to see, it is also hard to focus, hard to make out
details; before you know it you are walking down the wrong path
or right past a friend without noticing. Opportunity might be right
in front of you, but your vision is so blurry that you can't see it, so
you let opportunity pass you by. Surviving and thriving are
instinctual, but they are also based on where you are and where
you want to be. If you make those two things—where you are and
where you want to be—the eyeglasses that you see the world

through, then you'll *do* what is necessary to survive and thrive.

The same way hunger sits in your belly, where you are now and

where you want to be in the future should be in front of your eyes

so you see them every day when you observe the world around

you.

A teenager with a blurry vision might say, "No, I'm not

going to be a waiter, what will I gain from that?" Meanwhile, a

teen with a clear vision will take those jobs out of necessity, then

they will build up their communication skills, character, integrity,

discipline, and experience. Furthermore, there might be an

opportunity while waiting those tables that the clear-visioned teen

receives but the blurry-visioned person does not. The clear-

visioned teen might dream of becoming a well known singer, they

might record music on their time off, and then while waiting

tables, they meet someone who is in the music industry and can

mentor them— there goes an opportunity; meanwhile the blurry-

visioned teen lost that opportunity altogether.

The interesting part of this concept is that you might look at some people you meet who do things based on necessity and you might think that their vision is blurred, or you might even think that of yourself. "They are unintelligent, losers, unsophisticated and lost. How can they have clear vision?" you might think, but you'd be missing the point. We all begin life with a clear vision, because we are creatures of survival—remember the animals with literally the clearest vision in the world are birds of prey, such as eagles, hawks, and owls. But throughout our lives, our vision gets blurred because we get easily distracted. We get distracted with the fancy, the fake, and the foolish so we can't focus on what's important.

The person who is surviving, who is *doing*, who is tied to what it means to survive, is the person with the clearest vision. But that vision certainly doesn't mean he or she is without flaws; ones clear vision needs to be expanded on in order to see the bigger picture in a situation and gain more knowledge.

The person with blurred vision puts their family in harm's way, they want things handed to them, they want easy money, they want something for nothing, and the worst of all, sometimes they get something for nothing but then lose it because they never developed the muscles of survival.

In order to be a person with clear vision, you must work hard every day, you must do every day, you must strive every day. You will have to understand the principle of surviving and thriving: if you don't do A, then you won't get B. If you don't cook or buy food, then you won't eat; if you don't work, then you won't have money; if you don't rob that bank, then your chances of going to jail for robbery are lower.

Birds of Prey

People with clear vision are birds of prey, they learn how to adapt, how to observe, how to survive, how to deal, and how to communicate with others. Let's face it, as social beings, we come in contact with each other daily. It's how we survive. Commerce doesn't work without communication among people, so learning how to best communicate with others will help you survive and thrive. It will teach you how to be more **d**isciplined, how to maneuver socially hazardous environments, and **d**eal with the emotions of others. But a person with a blurred vision will easily go through life walking away from uncomfortable situations. They will not last long and will definitely not see the realization of their **d**reams.

The husband and wife team behind Forever 21 did not always have it easy when they moved to the U.S. from Korea. Jin Sook and Do Won "Don" Chang came to the U.S. with no money, no college degrees, and no jobs. What they didn't do was complain, play around with fancy materialistic items, try getting something for nothing, or waste their time and money on fleeting desires. Instead, they had the clear vision of the hawk—if they didn't work, they didn't survive—and so they started working three jobs to make ends meet before they opened up their first store.[14]

If our existence spans a few million years and is shaped by our ability to survive by exploiting our land, then we have to understand that this experience is one of survival. We were hunters and gatherers because we needed to hunt and gather to survived and thrive, we were farmers because we needed to farm to survive and thrive, we were specialists in crafts because we needed to specialize to survive and thrive, we worked through the industrial revolution because we needed jobs and industry to survive and thrive, we fought for civil rights because we needed equality in order to survive and thrive, and guess what? As we are still humans, the principle remains the same, we are survivors first and foremost. This survivor's mentality is what you need to adopt. While other people metaphorically have 20/20 vision, those who

---

[14] Elkins, Kathleen. "From Pumping Gas to a $6 Billion Fortune - the Impressive Rags-to-Riches Story of Forever 21's Husband-and-Wife Cofounders." *Business Insider*, Business Insider, 12 May 2015, www.businessinsider.com/rags-to-riches-story-of-forever-21-cofounders-2015-5.

adopt the survivor's mentality, with the eye of the hawk, have 15/15 vision—past perfect.

People who understand the formula for surviving and thriving see their older selves years beforehand; in their 20s, they are telling themselves that what they do right now will translate into who they become at 40, 50, and 60. It gives them a process. This simple survive and thrive mentality grows into surviving and thriving in relationships, businesses, crafts, money management, and all other fields. This formula, in its most basic form, is the same—find out what you have to do in order to survive and do it. It seems simple, but the work is always hard.

For example, you may be working in retail, and while working, you see a customer who appears successful pass by you. You can ignore them, but if you understand that in order to survive and thrive you must learn from the successes of others, you will go and speak with that successful person to learn. If you are shy, then you can get over that weakness because the desire to be successful is more important than the feeling of shyness. There are people who were terrible at cooking when they were young, but as they got older, they became great chefs. Why? Because they had to learn how to cook in order to survive.

Success is like nutrition—the same way you eat every day, you should work on success every day. Working on success can be reading, earning money, getting an education, living healthy, and producing something that makes you proud. Every day you must *do*. You don't have time to waste. Sure, you can go to parties, but are those parties adding to your overall success in life? Are you partying because it makes you happy? Or are you partying to be destructive? Knowing what you like and what makes you happy is a helpful part of success because it lowers your stress levels, and less stress helps you focus better. So it's okay to do things that make you happy.

There should be no days off. If you are not *doing* something every day to be successful then you are metaphorically starving yourself. Even if you work on your success just a little bit on a layback day, you are still feeding yourself something, instead of going malnourished for that day.

Honestly, if you are doing something for your success but it fails, it's still a source of nourishment because you are learning what you did wrong and how you can fix it moving forward.

12. Desire

When your desires are strong enough, you will appear to possess superhuman powers to achieve. - Napoleon Hill

Taking action isn't a one time thing, taking action is a consistent effort. Every day you must **do**. Along that process you will face a lot of obstacles and challenges. Once you reach those obstacles, you will need certain Ds to get past them. The first D you'll need is desire, because out of all the Ds, your desire is going to keep you active and awake. This is why it's important to remind yourself of your desire on a daily basis.

So let's say you **d**iscover yourself, you have a **d**ream, you create your **d**esign, you make the design **d**etailed, you know your **d**irection, and you act; now you must combat the obstacles that come in your way. There will always be obstacles, you can not change that, but you can change the way you react to the obstacles. Let's say you want to lose weight; you try a weight loss routine for a week, but you slack off because you get busy with other things, then you eventually stop. Stopping means your desire is not strong enough.

In the previous chapter, you learn that some of these people who embody action have a desire that is greater than any circumstance. It's simple, they have no choice but to *do* in order to survive, and their desire to survive is greater than their circumstances; similarly, their desire to be successful is greater than their circumstances.

Your desire has to be greater than any obstacle. Think about this, your stomach grumbles and rumbles. Why? Because your body has its own desires—your body wants food and nourishment. That same idea of desire is applicable to all other parts of life. Your mind wants nourishment too, so you might read, learn, and/or go to school. In order to support yourself, you have to look for work. You may look for work and get disappointed after a few attempts, but if your desire to adequately support yourself is greater than the few failed attempts, you'll continue searching.

You can acknowledge that the act of *doing* is tied to survival. Doing something for one day will get you through that one day, but doing something constantly is surviving and thriving. It's like the old saying, "if someone gives you a fish, you can eat for a day, but if someone teaches you how to fish, you can eat for a lifetime."

In order to *do* constantly, you'll need to tap into your desires. Now what is desire?

All desire—physical, mental, emotional, spiritual, financial—begins with instinct, experience, and/or comparison. On one end of the spectrum is the instinctive desire for something, such as food, sleep, play, protection, and love; on the opposite side of the spectrum is the desire caused by comparison—you compare what you have to what you see others with; and in the middle of the two extremes is the desire that comes from our positive experiences with things and our interest in experiencing those things more. A child will desire a coat because she feels cold (instinctive), then she sees another coat which she thinks looks nicer than hers, so she desires that coat instead (comparative), after experiencing a certain kind of coat, whether it's her old or new coat, she may like the coat's features, get familiar with the coat, and desire that specific coat (experience).

But how can desire overcome obstacles? Our minds control our desires without much effort through comparison—when we see someone who we think is in a better position than we are, our minds automatically compare and contrast. Then we make decisions based on these comparisons and contrasts. Your job is to control your mind and manually, instead of automatically, compare and contrast yourself to someone who is successful at what you want to do. For example, if your goal is to become a great salesman, find out what great salesmen have done, and desire to do what they did, but better. Surround yourself with the deeds, sayings, and ideas of great salesmen; learn how they interact with customers and emulate that interaction.

The thing about desire is that there is a tipping point. Desire can turn into a neurological itch, vice, and addiction. If we get greedy, glutinous, lustful or addicted, we can destroy any hope of success. You certainly want to be obsessive about the goal to an extent, but you don't want to spend an unhealthy amount of time focusing solely on one factor of the goal or you'll go mad. If you go mad, you won't be able to focus on your success.

In order to assure that you don't become obsessive about one factor, focus on various factors of the goal. For example, if you want to be a great salesman, don't only focus on the advice of one great salesman; read, listen to, and learn about a bunch of great salesmen. Try gaining experience from observing other things. Think outside of the box—get fresh air, try new experiences. Though your desire is to become a great salesman, read books and watch shows that seemingly have nothing to do with sales, and try learning about sales from them. I regularly watch the Discovery Channel not just for entertainment but to improve my sales skills by learning about survival skills.

What you desire should always be greater than the obstacles in front of you, or else you don't really desire it.

<u>13. Drive</u>

Set out with some definite purpose in life and accomplish that purpose. There is little that the human mind can conceive that is not possible of accomplishment. The thing to do is to make up your mind what you are going to drive for, and let nothing stand in the way of its ultimate accomplishment. - Charles Schwab

Once your desire is greater than your obstacles, you can overcome

them because if there's something in the way of you and your

goals, naturally you will *desire* to get rid of it so you can reach

your goals. But let's say you overcome one challenge, then

multiple challenges appear; how will you keep yourself motivated?

If one challenge weighs you down, how will you free yourself

from it? What happens when the flame of that desire starts to

dwindle? For instance, Michael Phelps desired to be the best

swimmer alive, he never missed a practice for five years straight

while he was trying to be the best; but what about the days he

didn't feel like practicing? On those days, he had to do more than just desire, he had to *drive* himself.[15]   This is where you start

understanding the potentials of the human spirit.

The Origins of Drive - Evolution

Did you ever think about how you made it this far? You, as a

member of the human species, made it all the way to the 21st

century. Imagine you're in a jungle in South Africa some 300,000

years ago, and in case you were wondering, there are no books, no

cellphones, no currencies, and no possibilities of posting a message

on facebook when you are in danger. Your main goals are to

survive and thrive. One day you are out gathering fruits for your

tribe, when suddenly a huge brown saber-tooth tiger jumps out of

the bushes and runs at you. Think fast, what are your choices?

I'm sure you can try negotiating with the tiger, right? No, if you

want to survive, you will either fight or flight.

Our emotional reaction to either fight or flight is a staple

part of our human genetic makeup. It's a physiological reaction to

---

[15] CBSNews. "Michael Phelps On Making Olympic History." *CBS News*, CBS
Interactive, 31 May 2009, www.cbsnews.com/news/michael-phelps-on-making-
olympic-history/.

a perceived threat, or in this case, a challenge. Other characteristics like negotiation and persuasion show the intellectual capacity of humans to communicate, setting us apart from animals; but dealing with threats through communication does not come naturally to us, it is learned. What comes naturally to us is to fight or flight; that's why when someone disrespects you, your body tenses up and you immediately get a rush of anger, or when something heavy is thrown at you, you jump out of the way. The fight or flight reaction is one of the oldest human reactions, and we wouldn't be here without it; additionally, it's a source of some of our bravest and most creative achievements.

The first time our ancestors faced a challenge, such as a charging saber-tooth tiger, they understandably ran. But after they got tired of running, tired of seeing their family members mauled, and tired of hiding, they got smart. They used their brains to get creative and design tools—like spears—that could fend off the predators. The next time a saber-tooth tiger attacked, one of the hunters would use a spear and confront the tiger, thus accepting the tiger's challenge. Instead of running, he would fight back, proving

the strength of the human spirit to overcome challenges.

If our ancestors never faced the challenges of their predators, they

never would have reached their potentials and as a result,

      1. They never would have **d**eveloped their creative brains,

and

      2. They never would have **d**eveloped the drive to fight

against their obstacles.

Drive Analyzed: Challenge, Competition, Commitment

Challenges shape our actions more than anything else. Human

potential is limited on it's own, but if it is challenged, then human

potential can break through its limitations. Many things can

challenge you, but the most long lasting challenge is *yourself.* You

shouldn't step up to a challenge only when someone challenges,

doubts, or hurts you, but you should be challenging yourself on a

continual basis. When other people challenge you, there should be

two challenges: the challenge the other person gives and the
challenge you give yourself. That is what separates good from
great. Understand that if you're only driven when others challenge
you, you will be a servant to them, whether you win or lose,
because if you make them solely your driving force, then when
they are gone, you won't have any drive.

The greatest people in the world would have been great
doing anything because they had an internal drive to do it—they
challenged themselves more than anyone else challenged them.
Sure their family, mentors, and peers challenged them along the
way, but when fire tests gold, it's still testing *gold*, and the value is
still going to be high regardless. Usain Bolt has coaches and
competitors that challenge him, but he shows up to practice every
day even when he is slacking, he puts in 120% with or without his
coaches and competitors.[16] When the coach isn't there he is still
training. Every day he tries to beat his previous time. Whether his
coach is challenging him or he is challenging himself, he has two

---

[16] Bolt, Usain, and Matt Allen. *Faster than Lightning: My Autobiography*.
HarperSport, 2014.

decisions, he can either accept the challenge or he can walk away from it. What choice do you think he made?

Competition

Bolt's competitors are the best in the world, so if he wants to be a world-renowned champion, he has to defeat these competitors. Fire tests gold the way competition tests man.[17] Drive increases with competition. Whether a man challenges himself or not, competing can drive him to his greatest accomplishments. Having a like-minded competitor at your heals or in front of you can give you a reason to win, just as a predator and prey compete against each other for survival. The more you compete, the better you become, and by the end of your lifetime, you will have done and still be able to do things that people think are impossible.

I'm convinced that Usain Bolt would have been good at any profession because he challenged himself and he continues to challenge himself, but he would certainly be someone else without competition. Competition brings out a different beast in people.

---

[17] Seneca, *De Providentia* (On Providence): cap. 5, line 9.

We can be content with laziness, but when that saber-tooth tiger shows up, when that hurricane strikes, when a competitor is in the way of our goals, we immediately jump into action because we want to survive and thrive.

If you want to reach your greatest potential, compete. Competing once isn't enough, you can defeat your competition one day, then lose the next. That's not how champions are made. If you want to overcome obstacles, if you want to tap into your drive, then you must harness the competitive spirit and compete every day. If you need someone to compete against during practices, you can always compete against *yourself.* Compete against your old record, compete against your doubts, compete against the old you.

Commitment

Drive is a 24/7 commitment; it's not an every other day activity, you have to be driven at all times, even if you don't feel like it one day. Here's how you can do it: pick out your challenges, name them, and accept them. Find people who have accepted the same challenges in their lives, or who are willing to compete. Maybe your challenge is losing extra fat; find gym buddies with the same goals and challenges, and have a friendly competition with them. In order to stay driven, you have to make commitments and write your commitments down. How can you expect to lose fat if you have a refrigerator full of sweets and fatty foods? You must commit to eating good, while exercising on a regular basis.

When Usain Bolt and Michael Phelps declared their goals to the world, they committed themselves to *a work schedule*—training daily, eating healthy, and tracking their speeds. A driven person will make commitments that seem out of their comfort zone and impossible, but they will overcome whatever obstacles they need to in order to fulfill their goals.

The UFC featherweight champion "Notorious" Connor McGregor is a great example of drive. In 2016, McGregor seemed untouchable. He beat the best fighters in his division with ease—even the former featherweight champion, Jose Aldo, lost to McGregor in less than thirteen seconds with one punch.

McGregor **d**reams of being a champion, his **d**esign is his style of training, his **d**irection is within the UFC, he is **d**etailed in his training ãnd it shows in his striking, he **d**eclares himself a champion every chance he gets, and his **d**esire to be a champion is certainly greater than any challenge he faces.

But in the Spring of 2016, after becoming one of the most high profiled fighters in UFC history, McGregor accepted the toughest challenge of his professional career—a bout with Nate Diaz. At the time, Diaz was certainly McGregor's enemy in fighting style and psychological game.[18]

McGregor usually wages psychological warfare against his opponents, trash talking them for weeks at press conferences as an attempt to irritate them before they even get in the ring. Some say this is the reason Aldo fell within thirteen seconds of their fight. But Nate Diaz is a heavy trash talker himself, who is motivated by the negative energy McGregor throws at him. As for fighting style, Diaz is a well accomplished grappler, a jiu jitsu black belt,

---

[18] "UFC 196: McGregor vs. Diaz." *UFC*, www.ufc.com/event/UFC196?id=. Accessed 4 Sept. 2017.

and a high stamina fighter; meanwhile McGregor is mainly a

striker, which means his specialty is striking like a boxer, but his

grappling is weak compared to Diaz and his fights usually end

quickly so he doesn't have to exhibit much stamina for five rounds.

Additionally, McGregor agreed to go up in weight class and

Diaz agreed to go down for the fight. So McGregor accepted a

challenge from a fighter who is used to fighting bigger guys.

In their first fight, McGregor landed strong punches to

Diaz, opening a cut above Diaz's eye and seemingly damaging

him; but Diaz fed off of those strikes, and his stamina kicked into

high gear as he delivered heavy punches of his own. Eventually

McGregor couldn't keep up with the high energy of Diaz, nor

could he handle the dense punches Diaz landed, and soon, he fell

to a rear-naked chokehold submission and lost.

That's competition, that's what McGregor signed up for.

Thanks to that match, McGregor knows what humiliation feels

like. All the trash talking, all the fame, pre-declaring his victory,

accepting the challenge to go up in weight class, all just to lose.

There is much merit in the saying, "the bigger you are, the harder you fall." But it is an honorable loss if you lose to someone worthy of competing against. If you accept a challenge, either you are going to lose or you are going to win, but the true **d**efeat is never accepting the challenge in the first place.

Having that humiliation over his head, having put himself on such a high pedestal and then falling off, he understandably **d**esired a rematch; he wanted to prove himself. He received his rematch, but this time, he drove himself to another level, a level he couldn't reach without Diaz.

The challenge was on the table and McGregor accepted it. After accepting it, he had to work on improving himself to beat his competition; so he trained with the best jiu jitsu fighters who are heavier than Diaz. He learned how to take heavy hits and maneuver bigger fighters. He worked on his durability and stamina, he studied Diaz's specific fighting style. He left no stone unturned. He committed himself to beating Diaz and his training regimen reflected this commitment.

The McGregor who fought Diaz a second time was not the same McGregor who beat Jose Aldo. The Diaz fight spawned a new McGregor. In their rematch, McGregor lasted all five rounds, avoided getting grappled, and landed enough blows to win the final decision.

That is the power of drive. If you want to keep your drive on a higher level, then you have to accept your challenges, make commitments, and continuously compete. Most likely your challenges will be different from saber-tooth tigers, but they can be just as fatal if you do nothing.

14. Defiance

"There is only one god, and His name is Death. And there is only one thing we say to Death: 'not today'." - Syrio Forel to Arya Stark (Game of Thrones)

Defiance has a lot of similarities with **d**rive and **d**esire, such as the need for a challenge, but there are stark contrasts. When you defy something or someone, you are primarily defying rules. Defiance is only possible if there is a convention, order, status quo, authority, injustice, imposition or oppressor to defy. These conventional elements set the rules and the defiers set the level they are willing to go in order to break these rules. There are different forms of defiance based on the different rules and defiers. A rule that states only a certain race can use a water fountain will harm the discriminated group and benefit the privileged group. Malcolm X's form of defiance was more tolerant of violence than Martin Luther King Jr.'s, but they both were defying the unjust status quo. Similarly, someone who defies unjust laws is honorable, meanwhile someone who defies just laws is a criminal. So you must be mindful of your type of defiance.

Defiance is fighting against that which holds you down. If someone challenges you to a wrestling match, and you accept, your drive to win that match can be great, but if the person pins you and holds you against your will, you must either fight or stay on the mat. Staying on the mat is no option for the defiant mind. So ask yourself, what holds you down now?

Defiance in Historical Context

The Ds of Greatness is an exploration into the rise of the human spirit—this rise is not complete without defiance. In the 13th - 12th century BC, Moses and the Jewish people defied the Egyptian pharaoh by escaping slavery in Egypt. In 490 BC, the people of Greece defied their would-be dictators—the Persians. Fast forward through a history of defiance to the American Revolution; thirteen colonies drafted the constitution of a new country, declaring not only their independence but also war against their oppressor, King George of Great Britain.

Fast forward to Mahatmas Gandhi and the Indian Revolution, Rosa Parks and the Montgomery Bus Boycotts, Emil

Kapaun and the Korean War, Luddites and the Industrial

Revolution; even J.K. Rowling, the author of Harry Potter, defied

convention.

J.K. Rowling's Defiance

J.K. Rowling[19] went through a difficult period in her life before

she became a best-selling author and billionaire. In 1991, after a

ten year struggle with illness, her mother passed away from

multiple sclerosis; riddled with grief, Rowling then moved to

Portugal to teach English and start over. She began dating while in

Portugal where she married and had her first child, Jessica, in

1993. The turbulent marriage only lasted for 13 months.

Afterwards, she moved to Edinburgh, Scotland where she was

diagnosed with severe depression. If that wasn't bad enough, she

was on welfare. In her words,

> "An exceptionally short-lived marriage had imploded, and I
>
> was jobless, a lone parent, and as poor as it is possible to be
>
> in modern Britain, without being homeless...by every usual

---

[19] *Pollack, Pam, et al. Who Is J.K. Rowling? Grosset & Dunlap, 2012.*

standard, I was the biggest failure I knew" - 2008 Harvard University commencement speech.

While on welfare and diagnosed with severe depression, Rowling sent her manuscript to twelve publishers but was rejected by each of them, every time.

At the moment when Rowling started doubting her book, the publisher at Bloomsbury Publishing company and her 8 year-old daughter read the manuscript. The young girl thoroughly enjoyed the first chapter of the book and wanted to read more. As a result, the publisher decided to publish the book. After the book was published, it gathered national and international attention. When Rowling's fourth installment of Harry Potter was released, it became the fastest selling book ever. A book deal and movie rights from Warner Bros. transformed Harry Potter into a pop-culture phenomenon.

Rowling's story is a beautiful example of someone who exhibited a defiant mindset that broke the conventions publishers had set for fiction books. Though her world was filled with disappointment and failure, she decided to take an unorthodox route by sticking to what she loved the most, and it paid off.

"It is impossible to live without failing at something, unless you live so cautiously that you might as well not have lived at all—in which case, you fail by default." - J.K. Rowling

History is shaped by acts of defiance, people are shaped by acts of defiance, the human will grows with acts of defiance. Defiance is nothing without a convention to break; so ask yourself, what convention am I setting out to break on this journey? Conventions don't have to be big, they can be little conventions that you defy until you reach greater conventions. The convention can be external or internal, it can be something that is solely affecting you physically, mentally, emotionally, and/or spiritually. It can be the thing that is holding you back from obtaining greatness.

Maybe you think greatness is only for a chosen few, or you feel inferior to others, or you think you can never get a raise, or you have some bad habits that you think are impossible to break.

You need to defy these deep rooted thoughts in order to free yourself and reach your greatness.

Society may even put you into small conventions like stereotypes, unequal payment for equal work, discrimination, and pre-judgements, but these conventions are emotional designs that are not backed by rational truth. These conventions are built and broken throughout human existence, and if you want to succeed, if you want to obtain your goals, then you must have a defiant mindset.

First, you need to find out exactly what is holding you down and why and how. Then, adopt the mindset that there is more than one way to *skin a cat!* Lastly, break away from convention.

Think of heroes from some of the stories you've read or movies you've watched. I guarantee, at one point, the hero faces a challenge, where the hero has to accept the challenge and then drive himself to overcome that challenge. Even further, there is going to be a point where that hero is oppressed—held back against their will. Some sort of force always gets in the way of the hero and their goals. In order for the hero to overcome that force, to break out of that oppression, the hero has to be defiant.

Consider Bond, *James Bond*. Bond is widely known for being a defiant character—not just against villains but against authority. He doesn't follow the rules, and oftentimes, he goes against his superiors, but it is this defiant character that keeps him alive in every movie. He survives each threat by finding creative solutions. If he goes into a situation with a one track mindset, he wouldn't survive a day; instead he uses every resource available to accomplish his mission.

Yes, this is a fictional character but the human element of defiance is very real, or else we wouldn't appreciate it much—we wouldn't find anything empathetic to relate to in the movies and books. In order to defy your oppressors, conventions and limitations, you must understand that there is more than one way to skin a cat, and if people try coming up to you with singular answers or limits, defy them because there are multiple ways to

solve a problem—history will agree with you.

15. Diligence

Diligence is the mother of good luck. - Benjamin Franklin

Once you've defied convention, it's time to put in the work! It's 1998, and it's the last game of the NBA finals. The score is 81 - 83, your team is losing. You've got less than three minutes to help your team get ahead, all eyes are on you. What do you do? In this position, Michael Jordan, one of basketball's greatest legends, made two foul shots, stole the ball from the rival team, and then made a three pointer to win the game.[20]

It's April 13, 2016, and it's the last game of your career. With under three minutes left in the game, your team is down ten points, approximately, 84 - 94. What's the strategy? Give the ball to you. That night, Kobe Bryant scored exactly sixty points, and in the last three minutes, he scored over fourteen in order to win the last game of his career.[21]

[20] Halberstam, David. *Playing for Keeps Michael Jordan and the World He Made.* Broadway Books, 2000.

[21] Beacham, Greg. "Kobe Scores 60 Points in Unbelievable Farewell Victory." *NBA.com*, NBA and The Associated Press , 28 Apr. 2016, www.nba.com/2016/news/04/14/kobe-farewell-performance.ap/.

These acts of greatness aren't coincidences. They are the results of a great amount of diligence. Diligence is an uncompromising level of hard work, effort, and conscientiousness directed to a specific craft and/or occupation. Diligence is measured in time. For you to be diligent, you have to put an exorbitant amount of time in working on and thinking about a particular thing. It is widely accepted that in order to be an expert at a skill, you have to devote at least 10,000 hours to that skill. Of course that's a lot of time, but the rewards are great.

Great experts like Michael Jordan, Kobe Bryant, Al Pacino, Shaun White, Phil Heath, Marshawn Lynch, Elon Musk, Stephen King and many more have spent more than 10,000 hours working on their skills in order to reach a genius level.

Hardwork

If you are spending time on a specific occupation or skill, then good, but how you spend that time will determine if you are working hard. Regular work is whatever is necessary to get by, it's the common tasks; but hard work is going above common. Hard work is the work that figuratively and literally defies gravity, it goes against resistance. It's the difference between carrying a boulder up a hill and rolling a boulder down a hill. When you bring that boulder up the hill, the resistance training you get from that work makes your muscles and fibers stronger. Not only that, but your brain becomes stronger because you've learned how to fix a problem—such as how to maneuver a boulder up a hill. This is applicable to all hard work—hard work will make you stronger and smarter. The easier task, such as rolling the boulder down the hill, has mediocre to no mental or physical benefits.

There are no people out there who became great by taking on easy tasks. To develop strength—mental, physical, emotional, social—there is a level of resistance needed.

Effort

No matter how sick I was, how tired I was, I felt an obligation to my team, Chicago, to go out and to give that extra effort. **- Michael Jordan**

In school I didn't like the idea of effort, because if I did bad on an exam or paper, I would still receive an E for effort just for *not* quitting. It seemed so obnoxious to me, as if the teacher was saying, "Well, you didn't get any grade above a D, but at least you gave an effort for that D." Little did I know that effort would matter just as much if not more than the actual A outside of school.

When you fail at a problem, do you keep trying or do you walk away from it after the first attempt and try to escape. Effort consists of staying the course, of spending long hours to fix the problems that get in the way of your goals. Walking away from those problems will assure that you never learn how to solve them.

If you want to give effort, then don't quit. No matter how frustrating a problem is, work on it from different angles and take small breaks but always come back to the problem. What people don't understand is that this process of trying and failing will help you become a specialist on the subject. A specialist has to know a problem on a three dimensional level after long hours of working on it, so when the time comes to work on it again, the specialist

can solve the problem effortlessly.

Conscientiousness

We all get tired and annoyed, but what would our neighborhoods,

our transportation systems, our buildings, our homes, or our

livelihoods look like if all of us just gave in to our temporary

afflictions like tiresomeness, laziness or irritation? Don't get me

wrong, some people do give in to their afflictions, that's why

whenever you are making a judgment decision about someone's

work or an object's quality, you should examine whether or not

diligence plays a role—and more specifically, conscientiousness.

Someone who works conscientiously will think about the

reasons why they do the work in the first place. A conscientious

lawyer will think about the people they are defending, and they

will work long hours to assure that they present the best case; a

conscientious doctor will think about the lives they can potentially

help; a conscientious construction worker will want to build the

most sturdy buildings which will protect the people who use them;

a conscientious police officer will think about the people she can save.

Being conscientious about your work means that you are passionately working for the benefit of a thing or a person. People who work conscientiously believe that the work, no matter how hard, is worth it. This is why you have to really love the thing that is going to propel you to your greatness because in order to reach that greatness, you're going to have to work long hours on hard and resistant tasks, which will demand great amounts of effort even when you are tired or irritated.

So if you want to be diligent, you must be hardworking, show effort, and practice conscientiousness.

16. Dedication

At the end of the day, both men and women who become CEOs have showed tenacity and hard work to succeed in their careers. It takes not just skills but also extreme dedication and commitment. And regardless of gender, CEOs are measured by the same criteria - the growth and success of the business. - Susan Wojcicki

By now you should have a design for how you intend to achieve your greatness. There are two things you need to add to this design in order to dedicate yourself and see it manifest:

1. A social contract of loyalty.

2. The word **NO**.

Consider your design a social contract. It doesn't mean anything until you sign your name and, consequently, your life to it. This may seem too heavy for someone who attaches negative memories to the word *contract*, but that's just because contracts have a bad reputation since so many people have been screwed over by the other party in contracts; but in this contract, you are the creator and sole party, so the only person who can screw you over is *you*.

Contract

The most dedicated people in the world are those who have a passionate, religious zeal for something or someone. Throughout history people zealously dedicate their lives to ideas like communism, capitalism, democracy, theocracy, feudalism, and many more. Even further, followers are dedicated to leaders, fans are dedicated to artists, parents are dedicated to children, teachers are dedicated to their students, politicians are dedicated to their constituents, coaches are dedicated to their teams, citizens are dedicated to their countries, workers are dedicated to their employers and work—and vice versa. This level of dedication does not come in the form of a written contract, but a social contract of loyalty between two or more parties.

Parents sign a social contract as soon as their child is born; in their contract, parents are expected to protect, nourish, and provide for their child. However, the social contract works two ways; the child is expected to be obedient and trustworthy.

Your social contract is one of a leader and a follower—you are the leader and the follower. You cannot lead others without being able to first lead yourself.

You wrote the design you wanted; just as Moses parted the Red Sea, you created the path for yourself, now all you must do is walk through that path completely dedicated to it. If your dedication falters, your vision and the path you created will be overwhelmed by the crushing waves of life's stresses. Trust me, there will be stresses.

Our minds tend to go off track when we get behind on payments, fall on hard times, try juggling multiple things at once, or get angry. These stresses will happen, but your dedication must stay strong instead of faltering. On the contrary, this is when you have to believe in yourself the most.

Fear

If the work you do now is in-line with your goals, then it should be easier for you to dedicate yourself to the work because it's what you want, and if you don't dedicate yourself to it, then you can lose it, subsequently losing your dreams. But what if your job is a dead end that is not in-line with your goals, then you might be less dedicated. But, even if you dislike your job, you can still be dedicated to the money you receive because it helps you support yourself and your family; so of course you'll be running out of the door to make it on time for work, of course you'll make the necessary deadlines, of course you'll try to get by—all because of fear. You don't want to lose what you have, but losing money is a fleeting motivation. It gets tiring after you realize it doesn't fulfill you. You should be more afraid of not dedicating yourself to your goals than of losing things like money or status or reputation. If you ever want to see what regret looks like, visit a couple of people on their deathbeds and you'll find out. In life. you end up regretting the things you don't try, not the things you do.

You should be afraid of breaking your social contract because the stakes are high and the consequences come in the form of broken dreams—which no money, no status, and no reputation can fix. So no matter where you find yourself, no matter how difficult the road, stay dedicated to your path every day for fear of losing your dreams.

Say NO to Temptations

People and things will try to divert you from your path, but this contract should guide you away from those temptations. When someone tries to distract you from focusing on your greatness, say "no" however politely you want. Practice saying these words of polite rejection: "Sorry, I can't go out tonight, I have plans," "I have work to finish up later, I can't," "No, sorry, not now." It's simple, so don't overthink it. People and things can wait, but your greatness can not.

Say no to "easy" buttons! You know those things are fake, don't fall for them, use your better judgement. Say no to the 60 min schemes, greatness takes time and **hard work**!

Say no to the doubt! When people doubt you, or even when you doubt yourself, you need to realize that you are greater than the doubt, and you have dedicated your life to greatness, so when doubts enter your mind, tell yourself that it's too late and it doesn't matter because you've already decided to go where this

path leads. There is no turning back, no retreat. You are on a ship

that just left a burning island, the only place you can go is forward.

The same way you dedicate yourself to work in order to earn

money, you need to dedicate yourself to this contract in order to

reach your goals.

Create a social contract of loyalty for yourself and use the

power of the word **NO**!

17. Determination

Determination becomes obsession and then it becomes all that matters. - Jeremy Irvine

You may think that determination and dedication are similar, and you are correct; however, dedication is commitment to someone or something for a period of time, and determination is resoluteness of purpose for a period of time. You may be dedicated to your workplace but only determined to do certain assignments that interest you.

It's counterintuitive to talk about determination without understanding the root word—determine. According to Merriam-Webster Dictionary, to determine is to cause something to occur, so in order for you to be determined you have to cause something to occur. A determined mind is unreasonable in the end goal but reasonable in the means; how you reach a goal has nothing to do with determination unless you are determined to reach the goal through specific means. If I am determined to provide for my family, I can do so illegally or legally—which would be the more sustainable option.

Determination easily becomes an obsession; no amount of persuasion or negotiation will stop a determined person. So don't use this word lightly, because it has serious implications. Determination implies a lot of stubbornness and willpower.

Hungry To Achieve

If you are hungry to achieve something, and you decide to do what's necessary to achieve it, no force should stop you from trying. If a force—superior or not—is able to stop you from trying, then you are not determined. In this context, determination means doing whatever it takes to reach a goal. The idea of *doing whatever it takes* alone produces the greatest achievements throughout history. Achievements such as creating computers or sending a man to the moon cannot be achieved without a determination for the end goal; once you decide to reach a goal, you can find various ways to achieve it.

Necessary Steps

If you want to become a surgeon, there are steps you have to take; the difference between the determined person and the undetermined person is that the undetermined person will want to become a surgeon without taking the necessary steps; they consider these steps obstacles. So eventually, they will drop out of the program. The determined person will take those necessary steps, no matter how long or frustrating, and will eventually become a surgeon.

No Determination But Desires

As you go through life, you meet people who say they want to achieve goals but are not willing to do what it takes. Family members or friends may come to your mind at this moment, but just know that it's ok to lack determination for something you are uninterested in. People are not necessarily lazy for lacking determination with some goals, they may have immense determination for other goals.

You are reading this book to be *different*. You are reading this book in order to invest yourself in your goals—no matter what goals they are or when they come into your life. You are reading this book for guidance on engineering your own **d**estiny. So it's okay to be different than others. You want to be able to say that you work hard to achieve every important goal in your life. So be determined in every goal that you set out to achieve!

Excuses

I'm sure you've met people who make excuses—it's one of the defects of being human. We don't want to be associated with blame, we don't want to **d**eal with the negative consequences of our actions, nor do we want to deal with feelings of guilt, so we blame everything and everyone else. We make excuses like "I didn't make it to your birthday because of my dentist appointment." "Only if I was given a raise, I would have a better life." "That's just the way it is." Excuses nullify the success of any goal because if you fail, you can easily just blame the failure on someone or something else. But if you change your viewpoint, and see yourself as responsible for your failure or success, then you will take responsibility and muster the necessary determination to succeed. If you fail, you can learn from your mistakes and grow wiser and stronger. Don't make excuses, take responsibility.

The first university I attended in the late 90s was Fairfield University in Connecticut. I attended Fairfield and played football. I was great at football, but I dealt with a lot of racism on and off of the field, and I felt suffocated by the environment. Even the football coach treated me with disdain and a lack of respect. I made some bad decisions while at Fairfield, like getting caught with a bottle of liquor in a dorm hallway and punching a racist kid in the face. These instances tarnished my name with the football coach, and eventually I got kicked out of Fairfield.

My football career was over and one of my worst experiences was going back home without a scholarship, degree, or job. I got laughed at by old "friends" because I had nothing to show for my work. Instead of pointing the finger at my coach, the school, or my circumstances, for the first time in my life, I became accountable for myself. I decided that I would make a change and

I got determined to be successful!

18. Devotion

To succeed in your mission, you must have single-minded devotion to your goal. - A. P. J Abdul Kalam

You can always be dedicated to something or determined to do something that you are not devoted to, just like some people are dedicated to attending church every Sunday, but not devoted to the scriptures or the teachings seven days a week. Devotion is a way of life. If you are part of a religion, there are laws that you should be devoted to. In Christianity, Judaism, Islam, Confucianism, Buddhism, and all other major religions, there are teachings and laws, whether commandments or prohibitions, that you follow in order to be devoted. It isn't a one-day-a-week dedication, it's a way of life.

Devoted people often look past themselves and put their faith in a strong belief or higher power. A devoted member of any one of the most practiced religions in the world is devoted to things like peace, love, and charity. When times are rough even the most non-religious person will start asking a higher power for help. But asking for help is not devotion, actually giving **time and resources** to spreading peace, love, and charity and following the scriptures is showing devotion to a supreme being or religion.

You don't have to be a member of a religion to be devoted, but what are you devoted to? What and/or who are you devoted to? Those are good questions to answer, but they mean little if you don't actually spend your time and resources on those people or things.

You get the hint, the way to measure devotion is by time and resources—it's a matter of priorities. The things you give the most time and resources to are the things you are the most devoted to, period. For me, I give the most time and resources to my family and work, so I am the most devoted to those areas of my life. Then there are areas where I am least devoted, but still devoted, like my friends, community, and organizations.

There are professions that come with multiple devotions, where you don't just sign up to work for yourself or the organization, but for a larger mission. So, CIA agents are required to be devoted to both their work and their country; that's where they spend a lot of their time and resources. A firefighter is

devoted to their work and saving lives. A police officer is devoted

to their work and protecting people. A priest is devoted to a

religion and the people in the church.

Time Breakdown

If I was to give my devotions a percentage, 40% would be devoted

to my family, 50% to my business, and 10% to everything else.

There are twenty-four hours in a day. Science says that someone

has to sleep for at least 7-8 hours to be fully functional. So that

brings me to about 16 hours of consciousness a day. So 40% of 16

hours is about 6 hours; that's how much time I devote to my

family per day, which means I devote 8 hours a day to my work,

and about 1.6 to 2 hours to other things. Seeing as some days I get

only 6 hours of sleep, I occasionally have 2 extra hours to spare.

That was a simple breakdown of time, you should do the

same! We all long for more time, but too often we squander it and

wait until the last minute. Breaking down your time as I just did,

gives you a clear percentage of the things you spend the most time doing. Having this information can help you organize yourself, and change the amount of time you spend on things that are unnecessary while giving yourself more time for things that are necessary.

I understand that you don't always have time for family; if you don't have children, then you probably shouldn't be spending 6 hours a day on family anyway. Truthfully, more of your time should be spent devoted to your dreams. But if you do have children or loved ones who you take care of and you work extra hours to provide for them, don't feel like you're not devoting enough time to them, because you can still devoted resource.

Resources Breakdown

Let's face it, a big part of having resources is having income. But there are other resources that aren't based on money—like skills. People who can cut grass, garden, build, paint, plumb, install wires, and cook are extremely resourceful because they can keep a house together without having to pay others to do the work for them. Think about the resources you have besides your money.

For example, my non-monetary resources include my management skills, my sales and business skills, my network, and my strength, among many other things. People have different resources at their disposal; dance skills, artwork, athleticism, humor, community, wisdom, and handy work are all examples of resources. What are your resources?

I've already spent thousands of hours of my own time at work, but those thousands of hours include resources I devote to the work, such as my knowledge of sales and business, my network, my management skills, and my own money.

If you are devoted to something, you have to pledge both time and resources to it. If you only pledge one of the two, then you are only semi-devoted. Full devotion needs both. It's not enough to give only money to a cause, that's being semi-devoted, if you are devoted to a cause then you need to give resources and time.

I'm devoted to my child, so I don't just buy things for him, but I teach him lessons, I spend time with him, I utilize my resources to give him a well-rounded and enriched childhood.

Likewise, I'm devoted to my parents; I provide what I can for

them, and I spend as much time as I can with them.

Skills

To be very talented at something, to be a professional or an expert

at it, you must devote a certain amount of time—close to 10,000

hours of **d**eliberate practice to be exact.[22] I've spent that amount

of time mastering sales—so I consider myself, at some level, a

professional salesman. Furthermore, I figure I'm going to spend

that amount of time, or more, mastering the art of being a father

and a family man.

Being devoted to something makes you spend time and

resources; your skin is in the game. You might spend time doing

things you don't like, but if you are spending a lot of time and a lot

of resources, then whether you like it or not, you are devoted to it.

I would recommend being devoted to things you are passionate

about!

---

[22] Gladwell, Malcolm. *Outliers: the story of success*. New York, Back Bay
Books, 2013.

19. Desperate

I don't think human beings learn anything without desperation. Desperation is a necessary ingredient to learning anything or creating anything. Period. If you ain't desperate at some point, you ain't interesting. - Jim Carrey

Your resources and time are committed to your dreams, now you need to get desperate to achieve them. You see, read, and/or hear horror stories where the victims are absolutely desperate to live and the killers have supernatural abilities, such as black eyes or bodies that twist in unusual directions. Take Jason Voorhees for example, he went from being a human to an indestructible monster-like killer. If these books and movies showed horror and desperation correctly, then the desperate victims would develop some supernatural abilities as well. When the triggers or stimuli around us are abnormal or horrific, either we become desperate enough to evolve our abilities, or we lose. As far as I'm concerned, we don't truly reach our greatest potential unless we get desperate.

You've heard the stories, the acts of desperation that lead

people to overcome big obstacles, like Charlotte Heffelmire, the

girl who mustered superhuman strength to lift a car from

underneath her injured father and save his life. Or Chris Garner,

famed Wall Street stockbroker, who was in and out of shelters,

trains, motels and subways with his infant son, hitting rock bottom

and then getting right back up to eventually become a multi-

millionaire.

Desperate For Life

Here is a story you probably haven't heard because it hasn't been

glorified in the 21st century much: the story of Master Sergeant

Roy P. Benavidez.[23] Benavidez is a war hero and medal of honor

recipient whose life is a testament to the power of desperation

among other qualities like determination, diligence, and defiance.

As a child, he lost both parents at a young age and was adopted.

He became a troubled teenager, who decided to drop out of high

school against the wishes of his adoptive father. Eager to make

---

[23] Benavidez, Roy P., and John R. Craig. Medal of Honor: One Mans
Journey from Poverty and Prejudice. Potomac Books, 2005.

something of his life, he enrolled in the national guard and then

joined the U.S. Army Airborne School (jump school); he later

became a Special Forces Green Beret, one of the most elite special

forces in the world. In 1965, he was deployed to South Vietnam,

where he unfortunately stepped on a landmine while in action.

That injury sent him to a hospital in Houston, Texas, where he was

paralyzed from the waist down. He was told that he would never

walk again and would stay in the hospital until he received his

medical discharge papers. But he was desperate to walk. The

news on the radio didn't help his situation either; he regularly

listened to bad reports of the Vietnam War.

Benavidez was in emotional turmoil, not because he was

unable to move his legs, but because he was unable to go back to

Vietnam to help his comrades if his legs were out of commission.

Usually, desperate people want to stop themselves from suffering,

but this was a man who was desperate to go back to the madness,

he was desperate to fight for his friends, his people, and his

country. He was so desperate to help that every opportunity he got, he crawled out of the hospital bed, enduring excruciating back and leg pain crawling to the nearest wall to perch his back up against the wall and move his toes. Gradually, after some practice, he started moving his legs. After 6 months, his doctor finally had the discharge papers ready. But when the doctor came into his room, Benavidez jumped out of the hospital bed, ignoring the sharp pain going through his back and legs, and he told the doctor to look at what he could do. The doctor told him that just because he could stand did not mean he could walk, but if he walked out of the hospital ward, then the doctor would tear up his discharge papers. Benavidez struggled to walk, but to the amazement of his doctor, he walked out of the hospital ward, and his doctor tore the papers up.

Benavidez's brush with desperation had not reached its peak yet. In the next year, he would face a desperation so horrific that it could easily be the plot of a horror movie.

Horror

At his request, Benavidez was sent back to South Vietnam in 1968. On the morning of May 2, 1968, he joined a rescue mission to save a twelve man reconnaissance team that was sent in the jungle to recover enemy intelligence information. The mission would be, what Benavidez called, hell. He got off of the helicopter at a location about 75 meters away from the team. He then ran toward the team's location but came under enemy fire and was shot in his right leg, face, and head. He didn't stop to check his injuries though, he was desperate to save the soldiers. When he reached the team, he signaled their position with a smoke canister, and provided medical aid to them while securing classified documents.

After providing medical assistance, he carried and directed the team to the aircraft in order to leave; before the aircraft could leave, he had to recover classified documents from the dead team leader. As he recovered the documents, he was hit with a bullet in his abdomen and grenade fragments in his back. But even with these wounds, Benavidez and his comrades were still desperate to live. A moment of despair fell on them when the rescue helicopter

came under heavy enemy fire and the pilot was shot and killed.

A still desperate Benavidez secured the classified

documents, moved the team to a more secure area, administered

water, ammunition and first aid, and then returned fire to enemy

soldiers. He also called in tactical airstrikes in order to clear the

way for another rescue attempt. Again he was shot; this time he

was hit in the thigh as he provided first aid to a dying soldier.

Eventually, he put a few reconnaissance team soldiers on

the next rescue helicopter; but as he did this, he was clubbed in the

back of the head by an enemy soldier. After gathering his

composure, he proceeded to kill the enemy in hand-to hand

combat; during which, he sustained wounds to his arm and jaw,

leaving him with a locked jaw. Even with these injuries, he still

made two more trips where he carried wounded soldiers and

classified documents to the rescue helicopter. When he reached the

aircraft, he shot and killed two more enemy soldiers who were

rushing at him. Having lost a severe amount of blood and

sustained life-threatening wounds, he finally was dragged into the rescue helicopter, holding his intestines in his hands.

Benavidez was so filled with desperation that he exhibited superhuman attributes while trying to deal with the horror around him. Our understanding of what a human is capable of is limited; ordinarily, we go about our days wasting time and spending our resources on things that don't matter, but when our situation gets horrific and we get desperate, we can turn into super humans.

Mike Tyson, my favorite boxer, was a desperate man. Losing a match would throw him into a depression that he could not bear. So he did everything possible to save himself from those feelings, and that meant giving 100% effort in his training and fights; that mentality assured that he'd dominate the heavyweight ring in the 90s. A desperate person must have the mentality that they will win or die trying. I'm not telling you to literally die trying, but you have to believe that the worst will happen if you don't win.

Power

Desperation is powerful. The desperate have their backs against the wall, with the difficulties of life in front of them and the only way to survive is to push forward, to face those difficulties with grit. Desperate people go deep into the bottom of a hole and if they want to get out, they have to climb. Are you currently in a hole? If so, get desperate and do what it takes to escape. Spend the amount of hours needed to perfect your craft. Relentlessly target your goals; get desperate for life, get desperate for the lives of your loved ones, get desperate for the lives of your comrades, get desperate for success.

When the stock market crashed, I got extremely desperate. I made thousands of calls per week to get clients, I slept in the office overnight, I worked 80 hours per week, I wanted to survive! The desperation paid off when I locked in a client with $700,000 worth of stocks. But it wouldn't have happened without desperation.

I have a certain hunger in me that food cannot satisfy. It's the hunger to succeed. Do you have the hunger to succeed? Let time, death, sickness, despair, misfortune, and all other setbacks motivate you. They'll come into your life at some point, but you don't want to be on your deathbed regretting how you allowed these setbacks to get the better of you. You want to be on your deathbed happy and satisfied that you gave your greatest effort and achieved something, no matter if you failed more than you succeeded. Get desperate.

20. Defeat

I like to set up obstacles and defeat them. - Heath Ledger

As you know, your mind tends to rapidly go from one thought to another, without truly focusing on one thing. Buddhists have called this the monkey mind—the loose, uncontrolled mind. Whether you believe it or not, your mind is constantly at war with you. It's constantly giving you subtle suggestions that change the way you think, putting conspiracies and false ideas into your thought process, causing you to think irrationally, fooling you with the slightest doubts or the most sophisticated illusions. In order to defeat both your mind and your external obstacles, you need a foundation for doing these four things:

1. Controlling your actions

2. Living a placebo lifestyle

3. Digging deep

4. Learning how to deal

Control Your Actions

By controlling your decisions—making sure that you are not just acting on impulse but choosing your actions—you are being mindful of your responsibility at every facet of your life. Once this grows into a habit, you will understand more fully how your own decisions and actions lead to favorable or unfavorable results. Such as the difference between binge drinking alcohol every night versus a little bit of alcohol on an occasion like a wedding. The consequences of the former is that you have a higher chance of developing a need for alcohol and becoming an alcoholic, meanwhile the consequences of the latter can be a few hours of belligerence at best, but nothing as severe as alcoholism. Hopefully, you get into the habit of making decisions that will consistently yield favorable results.

In order to reach the point of consistent favorable results, you must think before you act and speak. People who lack control act on impulse every time; they blurt out and do anything, which is why they fail often.

If you can control your decisions by contemplating their consequences before you act, then you will have more control over your destiny.

As you know, I've faced a few obstacles throughout my life. My obstacles have held me down like a ball and chain, where I felt imprisoned. I'm sure you've felt that way at some point in your life.

But you're not physically imprisoned. It's not as if you are Nelson Mandela, who was imprisoned for over 25 years under an oppressive South African government. You, like the majority of us, get imprisoned by your mind.

You doubt yourself at times, your mind repeats the negative words of others, your mind causes so much emotional and physical pain that you can end up living a painful life. Notice how I emphasize that it's your *mind* causing you this pain, not what people are saying to you or the things that are happening to you. If you control your mind, then you can use that pain as fuel to overcome your obstacles. If someone thinks you are worthless, what makes you believe that you are full of worth? If you have

nothing that makes you believe that you are worthy, it's time to

prove to yourself and to the world that you are full of worth. Take

the negative energy and turn it into positive energy.

Before you focus on defeating any external obstacles, you

must focus on defeating the obstacles in your mind.

The Placebo Lifestyle

When an obstacle comes your way, your mind can fill you with

negative thoughts, it can deceive you into thinking that your

situation is a glass half empty. That is the worst place to be in

because that mentality will have ripple effects that cause mental

and physical health problems. You want to defeat your negative

mind so you can look at the situation as a glass half full. You have

to transition your mind from a negative outlook to a positive one—

always looking on the bright side. One way to do this is by

creating, what I call, a placebo lifestyle. I'm not just talking about

the placebo pill or placebo effect that helps you feel better, but I'm talking about the entire process of doing some activity that makes you feel better.

The Placebo Effect

The placebo effect is a positive effect produced by a placebo drug or treatment that is actually the result of the patient's *belief* in the benefits of the pill or treatment, instead of the actual substance in the pill or treatment—which often is sugar.[24] So if you're given a sugar pill and told that it will help you hold your breath underwater for longer, your belief in the pill will result in you actually holding your breath for a long time.

The first evidence for a physiological change from the placebo effect appeared in the late 1970s when researchers discovered that it spurred chemical responses in the brain. The responses were similar to active drugs.

Ever since the 1970s, researchers, like neuroscientist Fabrizio Benedetti at the University of Turin, have shown how the brain uses neurotransmitters to relay commands and messages to

---

[24] "What Is the Placebo Effect?" *WebMD*, WebMD, www.webmd.com/pain-management/what-is-the-placebo-effect. Accessed 20 Sept. 2017.

your body.[25] There have been studies which prove that placebos can increase dopamine—a neurotransmitter that affects emotions and sensations of pleasure and reward—in the brains of patients who are suffering from depression and Parkinson's disease. Patients who are given placebo pills or treatments reveal positive changes in electrical and metabolic activity in several different regions of the brain.

When lead placebo researcher, Ted Kaptchuk, Professor of Global Health and Social Medicine, studied the brains of physicians when they were working on their patients, he noticed the unconscious signals physicians gave their patients which helped them relax and feel safe.[26] According to Kaptchuk, "Doctors give subtle cues to their patients that neither may be aware of [...]they are a key ingredient in the ritual of medicine."

---

[25] Benedetti, Fabrizio, et al. "How Placebos Change the Patient's Brain." *Neuropsychopharmacology*, Nature Publishing Group, Jan. 2011, www.ncbi.nlm.nih.gov/pmc/articles/PMC3055515/. Accessed 23 Sept. 2017.

[26] Feinberg, Cara. "The Placebo Phenomenon." *Harvard Magazine*, 3 Mar. 2014, harvardmagazine.com/2013/01/the-placebo-phenomenon. Accessed 23 Sept. 2017.

In other words, the process of showing care for the patient plays a large role in the effect the placebo has on the patient. This variable in the placebo effect is applicable to your daily life. You want to create an environment at home of care and positivity— little things like kisses, signs of affection, hugs, and words like "I love you" reinforce an optimistic, cup half-full mentality. You'll feel better about your day when you create a positive environment and lifestyle for yourself.

The placebo lifestyle also includes the act of taking your mind off of stressful or burdensome things for a period of time throughout the day. Maybe you can try meditation, exercise, yoga, watching television, thinking deeply, hanging out with loved ones or friends, playing with animals, and stepping out of your comfort zone; try anything that will put you at peace by allowing your mind to escape everyday problems in healthy ways. It's important that you do this without using substances, like drugs or alcohol, because that is cheating, and it won't add to a long term shift in your mentality. Just as the person who cheats on a test doesn't build the intellect to pass the test with his or her own effort, you

won't build the peace of mind needed to defeat the negativity in

your life.

My unchecked loyalty for my "friends" slowed me down

from my greatness. I hung around the wrong crowds. I always

strove for something greater, but the people I hung around got

jealous and put their insecurities on me. One guy used to call me

"hollywood" because I strove for success, as if I should be content

with being average. Even though I dealt with this negativity, I was

still loyal to that "friend" and the others I hung around; I still

risked my own health and security for them.

Loyalty is a good trait to have for people who positively

influence you. But being loyal to toxic people will only result in

your own destruction.

Building Positive Routines

When you start building positive routines, you can face negative

obstacles and absolutely defeat them without an issue. An obstacle

like losing your job can be disastrous in your mind, but if you develop a routine of activities, such as meditation, exercising, participating in a social club, and letting your mind healthily escape or focus, then you are already working on fending off depression, which is a common result of a job loss. Depression thrives on inactivity; when you are inactive and unfocused, your mind can solely focus on negative thoughts. But when you develop a routine of positivity—a placebo lifestyle—you can optimistically focus on getting a new job. You have your health, you are active, you have people around you who love you, and you probably don't like your old job anyway, but this gives you the chance to look into other opportunities for career advancement, so your glass actually is half-full.

If you are a hardcore person, I'm not telling you to soften yourself, I'm telling you to be healthy. Some of the hardest people in the world practice positive activities and develop a placebo lifestyle that helps them reflect on their life and seek peace within themselves.

Obstacles

You must believe that every day you will fight. Some days you'll fight a weak person, other days you'll fight a professional fighter, but every day you will fight. You must prepare for the obstacles as much as possible, so practice your craft daily. Even when something or someone throws you off-guard one day, you should always be able to lean on your hours of preparation to eventually defeat the obstacles.

Again, if you want to defeat your mind and obstacles, prepare yourself, control your actions, create a placebo lifestyle, try anything that will put you at peace by allowing your mind to healthily escape the every day things and focus.

21. Deep

Believe in yourself, take on your challenges, dig deep within yourself to conquer fears. Never let anyone bring you down. You got to keep going. - Chantal Sutherland

Only a few people can defeat and control their minds. I'm sure you've seen athletes who fight until they burn out, and you've seen activists and warriors fight for what they believe in, and you've heard stories of civilians who exhibit extraordinary will and strength in order to rise above adversity. All of these people dug deep in life.

Mental Will

Chances are you've played a sport or game, or you've underwent some difficult labor at some point in your life. As you strived, you grew tired, your body got irritated, and you stopped before your goal was accomplished. Well it's natural that you stopped, you were exhausted, right? In actuality, you probably only used 40% of your ability.

U.S. Navy SEAL David Goggins has a scientifically-proven 40% rule for how to dig deep into your will power. [27] As soon as you feel exhausted to the point of quitting or stopping, you have only reached 40% of your ability, which means you need to keep going because you have 60% more ability left. So, when you get tired, you haven't even reached half of your potential. You've only just begun.

As you engage in strenuous activities, your mind sends signals to your body to tell it that you are getting tired. So you start showing signs of fatigue like the following: heavy breathing, sweating, irritability, self-doubt, fidgeting, and many more. But you are being tricked! You have more energy and potential in you than you believe. Your mind is only sending a "heads up" message to your body; but if you get caught in that initial message, you might think you will suffer or even die. Unless you are doing something extremely risky, the chances of you dying from going above 40% are slim to none. So no, you will not die, and no, you

---

[27] Itzler, Jesse. *Living with a SEAL : 31 days with the toughest man on the planet.* New York: Center Street, 2015. Print.

will not hurt yourself. That's complete BS! Your body is able to go the distance, you can go 100%.

You, and everyone else, are biologically socialized into thinking that those feelings of fatigue mean you should stop. When, in fact, you must acknowledge that your brain is tricking you, and you must keep going. When you start feeling weary, repeat these words: "this is my brain sending me signals that I am working hard and have only reached 40% of my ability; I won't hurt myself or die from this, but I will keep going"

The reason our brains send us these signals is rooted in our survival instincts. Back when we were hunters and gatherers, we actively ran from danger and hunted for food, but food was scarce. So when we ate, we had to hold on to the nutrients for long periods of time in order to stave off hunger, which meant we had to be inactive for long periods of time because inactivity would burn less energy. In order to make sure we saved energy, our brains sent the warning signals to our bodies so we'd feel tired and stop burning energy.

If your goal is to conserve energy, then listen to those signals your brain sends, but if you want to be great, you must ignore those signals while going the full 100% and above. If I stop my exercise every time my brain sends warning signals to my body, I won't lose any fat. If I quit managing my business when things get rough, then I won't be successful. If I had quit being a stockbroker in 2007 and 2008 when the markets crashed, then I wouldn't know my true selling potential.

If you can make it to the 40% mark, good start, but if you stop because you feel worn out, imagine how much of your potential you leave behind. When you haphazardly complete a project or activity, you cheat yourself, and you never reach your potential! You literally waste 60% of your ability every day, if not more, when you haphazardly complete things.

Thoughts turn into actions and actions turn into habits; if you create a habit of exhibiting 10% of your ability on a daily basis, you're going to be less than average. Giving 10% effort means that you are just getting by with life and letting things happen to you without control. On the other hand, if you exhibit 70-100% of ability every day, then you are digging deep into yourself and giving your best at everything you do, which will result in greatness.

RAAM

Imagine racing on a bike for one full week with 8 hours of sleep in total, living off a diet that consists of about 10,000 calories a day and 1 liter of water per hour, and working so hard that your hands and feet swell. If you can imagine those things, then you can fully appreciate Jure Robic, a slovenian ultra-endurance athlete and the 5 time RAAM (Race Across America) winner.[28] The RAAM is 3,000 miles long. It spans from the West Coast of California to East Coast states like New York, New Jersey, and Maryland, including the Mojave and Sonoran Deserts, the Great Plains, and the Sierra, Rocky and Appalachian Mountains. This track is an extreme test of endurance, especially because of conditions like extreme heat, fatigue, strain, hallucinations, monotony,

---

[28] Guillain, Charlotte. *Extreme athletes: true stories of amazing sporting adventurers*. Chicago, IL, Raintree, 2014.

dehydration, swelling, and sleep deprivation. For these reasons, RAAM is considered arguably the toughest ultra-cycling race in the world.

But how do competitors like Robic finish this extreme race? They go over the 40% mark. Robic developed a habit of pushing past the 40% mark and literally going 100% and beyond.

When Robic slowed down and got fatigue, like everyone else, his mind told him that he should quit; Robic actually tried quitting a couple of times, but his willpower to keep going was greater than his uncomfortable feelings. In addition, he had a very supportive team with him that gave him motivation and handled his schedule, including rest periods. His team told him everything he needed to do, so he could solely focus on racing.

By solely focusing on racing, Robic left the logistics of resting times and motivation to his team. In this way, his brain was not in charge of fatigue, rest, and encouragement, but his willpower and his team were. Not having to deal with the logistical work took a huge burden off of Robic's shoulders. It gave him tunnel-vision focus and a fanatical fervor. Digging deep requires a combination of willpower, tunnel-vision focus, and fanatic fervor.

Fanaticism

Deepness is the trait of a fanatic—someone who believes passionately with little analytical thought. I'm not suggesting you become a fanatic for an ideology or religion, but I am telling you that you must become a fanatic for something that will help you reach your goals, and more importantly, you have to become a fanatic for yourself—you have to believe in yourself.

When fanatics are experiencing the presence of their deity or ideology, they exhibit less activity in the frontal lobes of their brains where analytical thinking occurs, but more activity in the parietal lobe, the emotional part of the brain. The parietal lobe is good for digging deep and utilizing your willpower, but analytical thinking often comes with doubts and hesitations.

Willpower

Reason is necessary before you commit to an action; but once you've planned out the steps and committed to an action, you have to execute with more willpower than reason. In order to keep progressing from 40% to 100%, you need willpower. Think of willpower as gatorade; when you feel yourself losing steam, send a surge of energy through your body like a shock by thinking about the reason you started in the first place— think about the thing you are fanatic about. Drink some *willpower* for the electrolytes and carbohydrates that will replenish your system and allow you to keep performing. Sometimes you even have to shout to yourself so you can externally hear the voice of willpower saying, "Don't stop," "Keep going," "F***," and "Sh*t." You can curse the world, cry, speak gibberish, but you must not stop!

Tunnel-Vision Focus

Having tunnel-vision focus means that you don't see or care about the things outside of the tunnel, so you are completely focused on what's inside of the tunnel. When people and things try to tempt and distract you, you will be unfazed by them. You are not a senseless fish who takes bait, so why would you devolve yourself into one? When you are on a diet and you see ice-cream in the supermarket, do whatever is necessary to walk away from it, even if you have to breakdance. Don't give in to what's easy; you chose the hard life, you want to be great, so keep at it!

When the stock market crashed, I worked over 15 hours per day to build my stock book back up. I had to dig deep. I lost my girlfriend and my life, and I was depressed. But I gathered my willpower, got fanatic about my abilities, and developed a tunnel-vision focus. Even though the stock markets crashed, I was able to secure a $700,000 account, and the commission on that account kept me above water.

Remember to use willpower, fanaticism, and tunnel-vision focus to go past the 40% mark.

22. Deal

My parents were dealing with evictions and repossessions and electricity getting shut off, and I just realized that I had to get it together. - Dwayne Johnson

Let's say you've experienced all of the Ds so far and you're on a high now. Nothing can stop you, nothing can take from you what you earned...except a thief. There's a thief out there, waiting to steal your life's work, waiting to take a loved one from you or snatch whatever you hold dear.

This thief will quickly throw your focus off and move you from the top of the success ladder to the bottom in a sudden change. The thief comes in the form of a sudden change because it steals something very important to you by changing your life. It comes in the form of perils like severe injury, death, destruction, and financial downturn. These changes cause the worst experiences known to us—grief, depression, hate, madness, and despair.

Like a train, the conductor knows how to safely and punctually drive from point A to point B; he can deal with any challenges within the regular operation of the train, but if

something suddenly changes the regular operation, such as train

derailment, it can throw him off guard. Most likely, he will be

unprepared for it. However, if he has had the right training and is

prepared, then he can deal with the sudden change better than

someone who hasn't.

The same goes for you, a sudden change can leave you

incapable of carrying out your goals and reaching your greatness.

Instead of getting up daily to work hard at your skills, you might

find yourself depressed while laying in bed for weeks. What you

need is good preparation.

The Mind

Everyone is susceptible to the sudden changes of life.

There are some people who are used to change, despair, grief, and

depression. They have developed ways of dealing with them, but

those ways aren't always healthy. In fact, bad habits are usually

formed by the unhealthy ways people deal with pain. For example, binge eating, binge drinking, drug abuse, isolation, and blame are all unhealthy ways of coping with pain, and they make the situation worse.

In order for you to adequately deal with sudden changes, you have to understand that these changes are common; if your mind can negatively deal with pain, then it can positively deal with pain. Maybe you just haven't prepared yourself for the sudden changes that you will experience, so now I'm going to discuss ways to prepare.

What Happened to Me

There is a three step formula for dealing with sudden change or peril.

1. Before

2. During

3. After

In the *before stage*, you must prepare for the worst. Ironically, in order to prepare for the worst, it's best to research, learn from history, plan, be honest, experience suffering, and find joy in the worst possible scenarios. The *during stage* is where you dig deep and remember who you are. The *after stage* is where you develop yourself.

Before

When I was working on Wall Street, I did not expect a financial crash. I was on top, I had everything I dreamed of having. I barely saved money, I took huge risks, I bought expensive things—jewelry, cars, and clothes—and I lived an expensive lifestyle, never really considering what would happen if I lost it all, until that moment happened.

By not considering what will happen if you lose something or someone, you are blinding yourself to the reality of a sudden change in fortune. If I had prepared myself for the financial crash by researching the trajectory of the financial markets in 2006, reading up on the history of financial markets, creating a sound financial plan, spending less and saving more, then the financial crash would've been easier to deal with. Don't get me wrong, it still would have been tough, but instead of losing it all, I could have held on; instead of my bank account going negative, I could

have kept some money; instead of relying solely on my stock

broker income, I could have made income from other avenues;

instead of getting angry with my friends and family, I could have

been more understanding.

It's sad that humans have this belief in our own

indestructibility when we are winning, but only when we are losing

do we feel our vulnerability.

Be Honest

Don't you think it's a shame that we have to feel the results of

tragedy in order for us to make the correct decisions? We can do

amazing things; we challenge nature with our inventions, we

garner immense strength and intellect, but none of these things

should blind us from our weaknesses—our bones get weaker, we

get sick, we suffer losses and tragedy.

Be honest with yourself, stop running away from the truth.

If you are insecure, understand it and work on improving yourself.

If you are physically weak, work on it and improve. If you are mentally weak, work on it and improve. Faking it will only hurt you in the long run.

You can prepare for a sudden change by creating positive habits that help you live a healthy life—mentally, emotionally, socially, financially, and physically. You can build strong relationships, meditate, be active, be empathetic, eat healthy, and make positive memories while keeping the negative memories close by so you never forget them. Death is certain, so be honest with yourself. Someone you love will die one day, and you'll have to prepare yourself to deal with it. Collect as many positive memories as you can while your loved ones are alive; financially prepare yourself for hardships and make sure you and your family are financially insured. These are all good habits that will assist you in dealing with peril and you should practice them regularly, instead of only when there's a sudden change. Getting ones act together last minute is how people we thought were great go broke —financially, mentally, emotionally, socially, and physically.

What's your plan for dealing with change? Start planning from now for when something unplanned happens; I guarantee you something unplanned will, this is life.

Make sure you spend time with your loved ones before they pass away, make sure they know that you love them; make sure you are surrounding yourself with true friends; make sure that you are a true friend; make sure that you have insured yourself incase you pass away, so your family will have some support; make sure you do your best to protect yourself from injury, whether that means insuring your car, house, family, income, eating healthy and exercising to minimize illnesses; make sure you have studied your own mind and you know what makes you happy; make sure you take time out to think about and plan for what you will do when tragedy strikes.

During - The Sad Box

Positive memories are beautiful, they keep you in good spirits, and they can create a happy place for you, but alone they are inadequate. We all have negative memories that we keep stashed somewhere, such as a sad box. You need those negative memories

of regret, despair, loss, tragedy, hate, rage, and shame that you tried

to hide. You need to take those memories out to remind you of

your goals, of the obstacles you overcame and how you overcame

them, and of how you can deal with those obstacles in the future.

In this book, I talk about the memories in my sad box often

because they help me remember my ability to overcome obstacles,

but when I lost my money, car and girlfriend, that sad box wasn't

the only place I went to, I also went to a happy place.

The Happy Place

When I lost everything, I gave myself a couple of days to mourn.

I even had ridiculous thoughts of suicide. In addition to my losses,

I stopped exercising, I stopped eating, I stopped talking with my

family members, I stopped enjoying life. So I had to dig deep and

go to a happy place. I had to think of the things that made me

happy in the past. Having built my life around materialism, I was

distracted by materials when I thought about happiness. But when

I concentrated on the things that made me happy, materials and money were not close. My family, my friends, helping others, and giving back to my community made me happy. So after my bout with depression, I began working on little goals and appreciating my progress. I also strengthened my relationships with friends and family. I focused on what I was passionate about—business and helping others. Eventually, I started a business that helps people.

After

The Monday after a Sunday football game is the most important day for a football team; it's the reflection day, the quarterback check. The football team is supposed to reflect on the game and figure out where they went wrong or right and how they can improve. This is the same thing you should do after every sudden change. Reflect on how you dealt with that change and what you could have improved on, so the next time something similar happens, you'll know how to deal with it.

You've got to understand that with every loss, there is an opportunity for you to gain something—maybe a new perspective on life, new opportunity, or self-knowledge. When you gain that thing, be grateful for it. Even with the death of a close family member; you can never get that family member back, but the stories you can communicate with your family about your deceased loved one are therapeutic. You can take a week to mourn your loss, but that person would want you to keep on fighting for your greatness. You should use that sadness to drive you to your greatness.

Take the things that family member taught you and hold them dear to your heart; communicate those stories and lessons to others, like your children or nieces and nephews. Do the same thing with all other pains; that way, those stories and lessons can help new generations keep the deceased alive.

Even now, my little baby boy gives me great happiness, and I can honestly say that a part of it is because I've experienced sudden changes like loss and depression. I value the time I get to spend with him more and more every day.

23. Demand

The game is my wife. It demands loyalty and responsibility, and it gives me back fulfillment and peace. - Michael Jordan

When there is a high demand for a good or service, people are willing to pay the cost—expensive or cheap—for that good or service. The supply for that good or service will have to meet the demand, but when the supplier is limited, the market for different types of the same supply opens up to new suppliers and competition grows. As competition grows, so does general wealth. But if there is no demand, then no progress can be made.

There would be no financial marketplace if people didn't demand it, and there would be no financial institutions, like banks, if people didn't need help managing their money. Demand for a more discreet way of transportation was how the taxi market opened up to companies like Uber Lyft, and Moovin. Just as in the marketplace of goods, you have to demand greatness from yourself and your circle. Not only must you demand it, but you must be willing to pay what it costs in blood, sweat, tears, time, and money.

The universe has the supplies and resources you need, but you must demand from the universe what you want.

When building a house, the building material is always available, but it's up to you to use it; different cultures use what's available to them. Some cultures cut bricks and steel, mix cement, and chop wood for their house, while others mold clay and mud, and tie bamboo and grass for theirs. As I write this, I am building my own house from the ground up; every day I learn how to demand greatness from myself and my team. Thankfully, the materials I need for success are all around me. I can find the information I need in the newspaper, television, and internet. I can find and vet the workers I need from my neighborhood, and I can search for the tools I need or create them. I actually just learned how to make cement last week! I demanded greatness out of my workers, and last week, they disappointed me by getting too comfortable, so I fired them. Now the next crew I bring in will know that I am not just demanding things with my voice, but I am demanding things with my actions. I am designing and building this house in my image by demanding greatness from myself and my workers.

How to Demand

If it's hard to find something you need or want, demand it so much that it is created, or create it yourself. How do you demand? You must organize, get serious, protest what's wrong, critique what needs to change, support what you like, boycott what you dislike, lead by example, join a group of like-minded people who demand the same things you do, use the resources you have to demand what you want, be uncompromising in your demands, be dedicated and determined to accomplishing your goals.

Most of our demands are for our self-improvement. We need to demand greatness from ourselves by organizing ourselves, getting serious about our lives, critiquing ourselves, supporting the things that lead us to greatness, boycotting the things that lead us to average, joining groups that will uplift us, and working on self-improvement. If you are reading this book, you are already demanding greatness from yourself, but you must continue.

The minimum wage of today would be considered

pennies, just as it was during the industrial revolution, if worker

unions did not aggressively demand higher wages. We complain

about the current minimum wage in America, meanwhile it could

be 100 times worse. Thankfully, people demand change.

Depending on the circumstance, your demand can be aggressive or

friendly, but it should always be serious. If your goal is to receive

a wage increase at work, and you know you deserve it, then get

serious. Don't be aggressive to your boss, but be serious. Demand

great work performance from yourself, and after some time,

politely demand meeting with your boss to request a promotion

based on your performance.

War on Mediocrity

Mediocre people do not demand much from life, they are satisfied

with whatever. The enemy of greatness is mediocrity. If you want

to stop being mediocre, you must dislike mediocrity, you must

show effort, you must constructively and regularly critique

yourself; you must be fully involved in your goals, not halfway.

Mediocrity is putting a quarter or half of your effort into something. Greatness, on the other hand, requires putting in one hundred percent effort. Being mediocre does not mean that you are poor or common or a loser; a mediocre person just does not want much from life. Our wants are shown in our actions; in effect, mediocrity is not showing much effort or giving much time to your goals. If you've decided on a path in life, you must demand one hundred percent of your effort on that path or give up now.

All of the great people I've discussed in this book exhibit the Ds, and they all dislike mediocrity. They don't dislike the sick or poor or common, but they dislike the substandard, half-ass effort put into reaching one's goals. If you ask me to train you and I agree, I will work with you the best I can, but if you start showing a half-ass effort, then I will not waste my time. You cannot expect to change your life or receive real results if you don't demand greatness from yourself every day.

At this moment, imagine your spirit coming out of its container and looking at your body. Critique yourself. Imagine your self demanding that you put more effort in your goals. Imagine your spirit demanding that you fix your flaws. Imagine your spirit demanding that you exercise every day and eat healthier.

Mother Teresa said, "if you cannot feed hundreds of people, then feed one."[29] But that is no excuse to be mediocre. If you can only feed one person, then do so *greatly*. A mediocre person would promise to do something but make up excuses for why it doesn't get done or get done well. A mediocre person, without much, would feed one person every now and then with crumbs, meanwhile a great person, also without much, would feed one person every now and then with a good meal.

Demand more from yourself, don't be mediocre. Moreover, you aren't the only one who demands things, but the occupations you want to be great in demand a level of work from

---

[29] Spink, Kathryn. *Mother Teresa: an authorized biography*. New York, HarperOne, 2011.

you that you must be willing to meet. If you want to be a great

singer, the music industry demands a great level of talent, hard

work, hit songs, and entertainment. If you want to be a great

acrobat, the sport demands a high level of dedication, practice, and

flexibility. This goes for all occupations.

Demand from yourself and your environment, and you will

receive the resources you need to be great!

24. Develop

Ever since I was a child I have had this instinctive urge for expansion and growth. To me, the function and duty of a quality human being is the sincere and honest development of one's potential. - Bruce Lee

The formula you have so far is a formula to plan your greatness and then overcome the obstacles that will undoubtedly come in your way. If you follow the D's up to this point, then you gain knowledge on how to be successful for a specific time, but times change. If this is a video game, you just learned how to effectively beat the first level of the game, but you need a system of development that is going to get you from the first level to the second, third, fourth, and final levels.

Who you are at age five is different from who you are at age fifteen, and who you are at fifteen is different from who you are at forty. As you grow, you gain more experience, and you face more challenges. You are constantly transforming, whether physically, mentally, emotionally, socially, or financially. The world around you constantly changes, so change is definite. You will transform regardless of your desires, but if you don't control

your transformation, you will eventually transform into someone

you dislike. Assure that your transformations are transformations

in upward development by learn from your failure, work hard at

your craft, being curious, and being open to opportunity.

Failure

Failure is probably the single most important experience you need

to develop yourself. When you fail, you are forced to look at your

shortcomings and figure out ways to fix them. Failure forces you

to become a problem solver, and in that process of solving a

problem, you are developing yourself. Life is like math, when you

fail at a problem but you keep trying, you will eventually solve it,

and the more problems you solve, the more you develop yourself

into a master at problem solving. In math, you become a

mathematician, but in life, you become a master in your field.

Before I became a stockbroker, I failed miserably at

numerous endeavors. I failed at becoming a professional football

player, a good student, a real estate agent, and a business man;

however, with each failure, I reflected and learned different

approaches to success so I could develop my knowledge and skills.

Ripley

Think about Robert Ripley, a world renowned cartoonist,

entertainer, entrepreneur, and amateur anthropologist, who grew up

poor in Santa Rose, California. He had bucked teeth, a stutter, and

wore mismatched clothing to school, so he was picked on alot. He

wasn't a naturally handsome guy, nor did he have the qualities that

would predetermine him as a successful man in the early 1900s.

But as a child, he had a singular passion—drawing, and he was

very good at it. He was so good at drawing that he made it a

serious endeavor. Right out of high school, a newspaper paid him

to publish one of his cartoons, and that's when he decided to make

drawing his career.[30]

Go Where There is Opportunity to Grow

Ripley failed at first. He couldn't get a job in his hometown, so he

moved to San Francisco where there were more job prospects.

---

[30] Thompson, Neal. *A curious man: the strange and brilliant life of Robert "Believe it or not" Ripley*. New York, Crown, 2013.

Unfortunately, or fortunately, he couldn't hold on to a job there and he didn't receive good enough pay.

Soon Ripley moved to New York, and this time around he developed himself more. He received higher pay per week so he started wearing nicer suits and found the time to play handball. This sport proved beneficial for him since he won a handball championship and developed himself into a better sports journalist by actually playing a sport and dressing better.

This was a guy who knew how to develop himself; every day he worked on his craft, developing ways to make his cartoons more appealing.

The Importance of Curiosity

Ripley's greatest trait, and the greatest trait for anyone who wants to develop him or herself, is a curious mind. If you want to be successful at developing yourself, you have to be curious. Ask yourself, what else is out there? What other opportunities will push me forward? What else can I learn about myself?

As a cartoon journalist, his job allowed him to tap into the curiosities of others through his own curiosity. He was curious about how his readers would react to oddities in sports, so he created a "Believe it or Not" segment where he wrote about a fun or shocking fact. People really liked getting out of their own reality bubbles to see something odd and unfamiliar for a moment, but afterwards, they wanted to go back to their own realities. As a result, his segment attracted many readers, so much that the greatest opportunity of Ripley's life opened up to him—the newspaper owner paid for Ripley to travel around the world where he was expected to write about foreign cultures and oddities for the newspaper. In a time where most people did not have the means to travel, these odd stories about an Indian man who could hang from a hook or the world's tallest human entertained U.S. citizens and made Ripley famous.

But he didn't stop there. Ripley developed himself even more. He wasn't used to being the center of attention or talking in front of large crowds, so when he accepted a deal to host his own television show, *Ripley's Believe it or Not*, he had a lot of developing to do. Thanks to constant practice, he went from being an awkward host, to a host as entertaining as some of the best hosts on television.

Ripley's success wasn't coincidental, he created a system of development. First, he worked hard at his craft, then he got curious, then he received an opportunity, then he worked hard at his modified craft, then he got more curious, received more opportunities, and the cycle continued.

No matter how far you reach in life or how passionate you are about what you do, there will always be boredom and monotony. So you need to develop a curiosity for life that will keep you moving forward no matter what. Learn from your failures, go where you can succeed, work hard at your craft, be curious, and be open to opportunity.

25. Define

Do you want to know who you are? Don't ask. Act! Action will delineate and define you.
- Thomas Jefferson

Define is the D which identifies the moment you become great. It is the defining moment of your life. Barack Obama's defining moments were when he gave a DNC speech in 2004 and when he became the president of the United States of America in 2009; his life was never the same after these events because at these moments, he stepped into the annals of history.

One of Peyton Manning's defining moments was in Super Bowl 41 on February 4, 2007 when he played for the Colts. He helped the Colts win the Super Bowl by throwing 25 successful passes out of 38 for 247 yards, and he became the Most Valuable Player of the Super Bowl. What's your defining moment? Have you reached one yet?

Defining Moments

Defining moments show up at different times in our lives. When someone writes and publishes a book, they become an author, but when they make the bestselling list, they become a bestselling author. When someone beats others at chess often, they become a good chess player; when they start winning championships, they become a professional chess player; when they beat the best chess player in a country, they become the best chess player for that year in that country; but when they beat the greatest chess players in the world, they become the greatest chess player in the world.

Throughout your development process, you will have defining moments. These are the moments that will change your life. Ripley defined himself as a sports illustrator, then he developed himself and defined himself as an entertainer; after that, he developed himself again and defined himself as a businessman. If you want to reach the next level of your life, you need to define yourself by developing yourself to that next level.

Billie Jean King

Another example is Billie Jean King. At a young age she defined

herself as a girl who was exceptionally well at tennis in the 1940s.

By the end of the 1950s, she defined herself as an amateur tennis

champion.[31] By the end of the 1970s, she defined herself as one of

the greatest tennis players—let alone female tennis players—of all

time. She played 51 grand slam event titles from 1959 to1983, and

she won the last 7 Grand Slam singles finals in which she played.

She won 67 professional and 37 amateur singles titles. She helped

the U.S. win the Fed Cup 7 times.

Her most remembered moment—a moment that defined for

the world that women were just as good at sports as men—was

when she defeated Bobby Riggs in the highly anticipated Battle of

the Sexes match in 1973 at the height of her career. Bobby Riggs

was defined as the number one ranking tennis champion in the

world in the 1940s, and he had gone on to become a promoter and

outspoken male sexist. So when Billie Jean King defeated him, it

---

[31] King, Billie Jean, and Frank Deford. *Billie Jean*. New York, Viking Press, 1982.

was an act of defiance and an opportunity for her to further define herself as a champion for women and to define women as equal.

Negative Defining Moments

Defining moments can also be negative. You become a criminal once you decide to steal, fraud, defame, vandalize, and/or murder. You are defined as a failure once you don't **d**are. You are defined as a worthy competitor once you dare but don't succeed. You are defined as a winner once you win.

My Experience

I was born in a neighborhood with limited opportunities, so the chances of me becoming involved in negative situations was pretty high. At a young age, I decided to hang out and do what I thought was cool, so I was defining myself as a mischievous kid; in school, I didn't take my classes seriously and I joked around a lot, so I defined myself as an ok student and a troublemaker.

I still made it to college, and I graduated with a Bachelor's Degree in Finance, so I became defined as a college graduate.

One of my most important defining moments, which pointed me in the direction I am in now, was when I defined myself as defiant. You may hear about how bad the 2007-2008 market crash was for many people, and it's very true. Many people who lost all of their money and assets committed suicide, so imagine being a stockbroker during that time where your income depended on stock performance. In a matter of days, I went from a well off man, to a poor man.

I came into the business when the market just started booming, and by 2005 I was making over $150,000 a year. Financially, I was successful. I made more money than my parents ever did combined. I was balling—I went to the finest restaurants in NY, paid for $400 dinners, bought expensive Jacobs watches, paid off two expensive cars, and got my passport stamped with plenty of beautiful locations. I thought I was invincible.

Then in 2007 the stock market showed signs of crashing, and by 2008, there had been a handful of crashes when the stock market finally bottomed out. It was a sad year for me. I went from making over $150,000 a year to barely making $10—I couldn't get

one stock sold. I had to sell my cars, max out my credit cards, and

go negative on my payments just to get by. I remember asking a

good friend of mine for $20 every week just to get gas.

My whole life changed when I hit rock bottom; my

girlfriend and I split up, I had to move in with my family, and I

started heavily drinking to cope with my problems.

How could this happen to me? A 28 year old college

graduate, making thousands of dollars, living the kind of lifestyle

people would only dream about, and suddenly, nothing to show for

it. The reality was that I could have gotten on my feet and worked

at a bank or some place where my experience would have gotten

me a job, but I chose not to, I chose to be **defiant**.

That process of hitting rock bottom truly changed me, it

helped me focus on my dreams more; as I struggled, I researched

everything I could find on starting a business. In the meantime, I

stayed at my firm during and after the stock market crash. I loved

the stock markets, and I wanted to pull through.

In 2010, I resigned from that firm and joined a different firm where I was much wiser with my money. I decided that I didn't want to deal with another stock market crash no matter how much I planned for it. Through a process of self-discovery, I learned that I love helping people and I wanted to start my own business in a field that was a safer market—so healthcare it was!

Every new plateau you reach will define you. Make sure you are the one controlling your narrative, and not someone else.

26. Discipline

Discipline is the bridge between goals and accomplishments - Jim

Rohn

Have you ever seen someone get angry because their phone died or their wifi took too long to load? Maybe you've seen people get angry because their train, airplane, or carpool got delayed. How about quick shifts from humor to sadness and/or indifference while scrolling through an Instagram, Twitter, or Facebook feed. Today's society is privileged; our privilege has made us victims of instant gratification, and as a whole, our discipline is faltering because we are so spoiled with instant gratification that the idea of waiting for something is foreign to us. But the process of waiting and delaying gratification is the mark of successful people. Unsuccessful people can't see the long term benefits of holding out for later or working on little daily goals to bring the bigger goals into fruition. Don't get me wrong, when an opportunity presents itself, you should act accordingly, whether that means act fast or slow. But if you are impulsive for every perceived opportunity then you'll easily start losing out—you'll lose your money by spending it on things you don't need, you'll lose your time by spending it on events and people who don't help you, and you'll lose resources by spending them on fruitless endeavors.

Discipline is the state of having control and order. Self-discipline is when you have control and order over yourself. So within discipline, other traits like patience and temperance are found.

Imagine you are waiting on a long line and you get irritated. It's difficult to be disciplined in those moments because when you are thinking about how long you have to wait or how bored you are, you will automatically get irritated. Your irritation can result in an overall bad day, and/or you might leave the line out of impatience so you'd miss out. But these are the perfect moments to practice your discipline.

Your brain will make you think that you are irritated when you are waiting, but it's really up to how you perceive your situation. You should look at this with a cup half full mindset. You can view the wait as an opportunity to converse, meditate, think

deeply, read, observe, play a game, and so much more. Instead of

giving in to impulse and temptation, discipline yourself by doing

anything productive besides unproductively irritating yourself and

others.

Discipline builds character because when you have a goal,

there is a certain amount of time you must devote to that goal.

Disciplining yourself means disciplining your mind, body, and

time, so if you must devote one hundred hours to a task for a

month, you will get the job done in one month. The problem arises

when distractions get in your way. Distractions are the true tests of

a disciplined person; they can easily turn your productivity from

one hundred hours in one month to one hundred hours in three

months, guaranteeing that you'll waste a countless amount of time

on things you don't need.

As with all of the Ds, discipline is an everyday task.

Discipline is a matter of being patient, having temperance,

controlling impulses, and working on your goals every day in a

timely manner no matter how your schedule turns out.

Patience

It once took six months to go across the Atlantic Ocean, and now it

takes a few hours. Yet, we complain about our flights taking too

long, as if our ability to fly in the air, something that was

considered impossible three hundred years ago, isn't awe-

inspiring. We complain that we don't receive the gratification we

are looking for on our phones—the same phones that can talk back

to us, tell the time, take pictures, videos, and thousands of other

applications with no effort. Scientists couldn't dream of this

device two hundred years ago, yet we wonder why we are not

satisfied in our lives. Look around you, there is satisfaction

everywhere if you are willing to be patient and disciplined.

Nothing kills satisfaction like instant gratification. This is

why 70% of people who suddenly get a large amount of money go broke within a few years.[32] Most people don't earn the money as accumulated earnings over time, so they don't know how to hold on to it. But someone who is disciplined in money management can receive large lump sums and still manage the money accordingly.

True satisfaction is connected to work and earnings. You must earn your satisfaction in life. Don't complain that you didn't make it to your destination on time, but love the journey and love the process. Besides, if you are well disciplined, you won't have to worry about being late because you will schedule yourself accordingly. If something else delays you, it's out of your control at that point, but you can focus on the things that are in your control, like your attitude and patience.

Temperance and Control

Few things threaten greatness like overindulgence and distractions. Plenty of celebrities have hurt their careers because they couldn't

---

[32] Polyak, Ilana. "Don't let sudden wealth leave you broke." *CNBC*, 1 Oct. 2014, www.cnbc.com/2014/10/01/sudden-wealth-can-leave-you-broke.html. Accessed 24 Sept. 2017.

restrain themselves from alcohol and drugs. Substance abuse is not the only thing that can ruin your greatness, but vices such as gluttony, greed, anger, pride, laziness, vainglory, lust, and any other vice you can think of can certainly take away from your greatness.

Why is Discipline Important?

If you are reading this book, then the chances are you have a goal in life. Let's say this goal is to be a doctor. In order to be a successful doctor, you have to go through training, which consists of a few years of school and then a few years of practice, and sooner or later, assuming you go through this process with good test scores, you'll become a doctor. But that is a heavy assumption. In reality, the majority of us suffer from metaphorical blind spots. We tend to look at where we are now and where we want to be, but we blind ourselves from everything in-between. Then when the process starts, a lot of us stop, or get distracted, or we realize that we don't really desire the goal.

Discipline will assure that you are successful in your goals because you will not be easily distracted by temptations, instant gratifications, and irritations. When you are disciplined, it's hard for everyday problems to phase you, so you are more focused.

If you think discipline doesn't matter, consider the doctor's office. Let's say you have an illness that requires surgery. I'm sure you don't want someone with low credentials working on your body. No, you want someone who shows a high level of discipline in his or her work—someone with high credentials, someone with proven abilities, someone who wakes up every morning to work on the specific issues you face. So if we demand this discipline from our doctors, because they help take care of our bodies and minds, then why not demand this same kind of discipline from ourselves, since we primarily take care of ourselves?

In The Zone

Stephen Curry, the 2015 and 2016 NBA Most Valuable Player Award recipient and arguably one of the best shooters in the league, owes much of his success to his discipline. In a 2016 interview, he acknowledges that his confidence on the court is a by-product of the amount of work he puts in during practice.[33] He's confident when he shoots high-pressure 3 point shots in games because he makes those same shots hundreds of times in practice; he follows a disciplined routine in practice. He says that when he is in a game, he is in the zone. He doesn't worry about failure or not making a shot because he has already made those shots hundreds of times, so it's natural to him. The same way talking is natural to you, shooting a successful 3 pointer that goes in while under pressure is natural to Stephen Curry. In the zone is where you want to be; you want to discipline yourself and practice your craft so much that it's as natural to you as talking.

Life is one big test with little tests throughout the years. One of these tests will be your life's purpose. A lot of people search for their life's purpose, but they can easily be misguided during their search. Your life's purpose is what you decide it will

---

[33] "Stephen Curry Interview." *NBA.com*, 3 Mar. 2016, www.nba.com/video/channels/nba_tv/2016/03/04/20160303-stephen-curry-kristen-ledlow-interview-v2.nba/. Accessed 24 Sept. 2017.

be. And that decision will not come into fruition unless you discipline yourself by working on your craft every day.

I suggest you work on your craft every day because you are only a mere speck in the thought of history so you really don't have much time to waste if you want to be great.

Imagine wanting to be a best-selling author, but having no discipline to sit down and work on a book every day; or wanting to be a movie director, but barely showing up to the shootings; or wanting to be a great singer, but not practicing daily—you will fail.! The disciplined competitor will easily outwork you. One does not gain 10,000 hours of practice time in a field by being undisciplined. You can't be a great basketball player, journalist, actor, business owner, or musician by distracting yourself with your phone or alcohol or drugs or anything that can sidetrack you.

Work on your craft daily, have patience, and get in the zone.

27. Dominate

I like to dominate 100 percent. I don't want to just beat you - I want to wear you down.
- Matt Harvey

Before considering domination, you should first understand self-dominion. I believe self-dominion is having sovereignty and control over oneself or a product of oneself, such as how a parent has dominion over his or her child.

Previously in this book, I analyzed what it means to have discipline and to defeat one's mind and obstacles. Defeating one's mind can be temporary, yet you have to exercise discipline over yourself every day; once you exercise discipline, you can have control over yourself. If you have control over yourself, you can have dominion over yourself. Having dominion over yourself means that you hold yourself in high esteem, you don't do things to appease other people, but you do things for yourself; you believe in yourself when others don't, you take responsibility for your life and your actions, and you know yourself inside and out. When you have dominion over yourself, you control your schedule, your

reputation, your work, your narration, and your decisions as direct extensions of yourself.

Once you have dominion over yourself, you can begin the process of having dominion over others. You can raise children so they have dominion over themselves, you can raise a successful company where you have to be responsible for employees, and you can manage an organization to bring about it's greatness. Some people who live in a free country or who get things without truly earning them don't understand dominion because they take it for granted; they are filled with indulgences and blessings that they haven't earned. But when you are vulnerable, or poor, or imprisoned, or hurting, there isn't much you can control besides yourself and your response to the triggers around you, so when you don't take much for granted, you can learn how to better maintain dominion over yourself.

What You Can Control

You probably hear the saying "focus on what you can control, and leave what you can't" often. So in any given situation, the things you can control are the things you have dominion over. I've discussed discipline and decisions in this book already, so by now you should know how to control your mind and reactions to the triggers and stimuli in your life. You should also know how to increase your self-discipline. In short, self-discipline and control over your reactions and mind is how you have dominion over yourself.

The more dominion you have over yourself, the more dominion you can exercise over situations. Having self-dominion is like building a strong fort and using it for protection in a war; an army can try destroying it, but if the foundation of the fort is strong then it's hard to penetrate. If the fort is hard to penetrate, then it's easier to protect your home and defeat your opponents when they are focused on attacking you because your fort is near impossible to destroy. As a result, you can focus on counter attacking your opponents when they make mistakes and get tired, therefore you are able to control your own situation first, then theirs.

More practically, when you have dominion over yourself, no matter what people do around you, you will always be confident in yourself and your skills, therefore you are less likely to be destroyed by pressure but you will exercise control over the things you can.

If you exercise dominion over yourself by controlling your mind and reactions and disciplining yourself to the point of being an expert in a particular field, then you will be confident when you are *in the zone*, like Stephen Curry.

Influential

People with dominion over themselves will always be magnetic and influential because they represent qualities others are lacking, like wisdom, intelligence, skill, happiness, wealth, confidence, strength, and the list goes on.

People gravitate to the things they believe they lack. So when you display true dominion over yourself, others will follow. Put it this way, you don't go on a plane or ship if you think the captain is a nervous alcoholic with limited experience, do you?

No, you want rational and responsible experts with dominion over themselves and their team to lead you to your destination.

When people are truly confident in themselves based on a mastery of skill and they can function well under pressure, they have dominion over themselves. Only then can they successfully have dominion over others because they have the foundation to lead others.

Parents have dominion over their children because parents have more experience in the world and have the responsibility of providing for their children; so more or less, parents are supposed to be good at providing and raising their children, which results in the children following the parents. Of course, not all parents are good at this job, not all parents have dominion over themselves, not all parents can exercise dominion over their children, but a certain level of experience in the world equips most parents with good child raising abilities.

The same goes for presidents and their countries, CEOs and their companies, leaders and their organizations, landowners and their lands, and estate owners and their estates; the person in charge exercises dominion over others. The mistake occurs when these individuals exercise dominion over others without first having dominion over themselves. In all of these situations, one can lose control. A landlord can end up with squatters; and CEOs and leaders can be expelled for misconduct, misappropriation of funds, and/or bad performance.

A lot of people will try to fake dominion; but they are frauds, and at some point, they are always revealed. So if you are fronting as if you are a leader or expert or confident or in control, then the truth will come to light when the pressure is turned up.

True dominion over yourself and others can then evolve into dominance, where you are dominating your field.

Amazon, the company, started off as a small online retailer for books in 1994, then it gradually grew into a company worth billions of dollars. The founder of Amazon, Jeff Bezos, and Amazon, as an extension, gained dominion over *self* by mastering online book retail and the company's trajectory. Then when

Amazon had enough money to dominate the E-Commerce market,

it began selling products other than books. Then it started to

control the shipping of its products, then it created its own

products, and then it bought up businesses, like Whole Foods, to

expand its dominance into other fields.

Now Amazon is one of the biggest companies in the world.

Similarly, McDonald's started off small. The founders of

McDonald's, the McDonald brothers, mastered their crafts and

practiced dominion over their company. Soon, they dominated the

area around the first McDonald's store in San Bernardino

California in 1940. Later on, Ray Croc, the famous McDonald's

franchiser, used the original McDonald's business model to

dominate the market and develop thousands of McDonald's

franchises throughout the U.S. and eventually the world.[34]

When I started my ambulette company, No One Left Out

Services(NOLOS), I had to start with one van. I had to establish

dominion over my company by learning the ins and outs of the

---

[34]Love, John F. *McDonalds: behind the arches*. New York, Bantam Books, 1995.

business with my one van. Soon enough, I expanded into multiple

vans and began dominating the area around me. But I didn't have

to expand, I could have stayed with one van. Even now I don't

have to expand anymore, but I want to because I **d**emand more out

of myself.

Dominion first and domination after is like a dot becoming

a small circle that expands. This concept of dominion first and

domination after can be applied to all other industries and/or crafts.

The music industry is filled with huge record labels, the food

industry is filled with big grocery store chains, the sports industry

is filled with athletes and brands that dominate those fields, and the

Guinness Book of World Records is filled with people who are

dominating their fields, however unorthodox.

If you've followed the Ds this far, then you already know

the industry or craft that will propel you to your greatness. You

should know where your dominion lies, and now you must decide

if you want to dominate that industry or craft. If you do, then your responsibility will be great because you will be very influential,

but can you *deal* with that pressure? Of course you can!

28. Dictate

Out of the night that covers me,
Black as the pit from pole to pole,
I thank whatever gods may be
For my unconquerable soul.

In the fell clutch of circumstance
I have not winced nor cried aloud.
Under the bludgeonings of chance
My head is bloody, but unbowed.

Beyond this place of wrath and tears
Looms but the Horror of the shade,
And yet the menace of the years
Finds and shall find me unafraid.

It matters not how strait the gate,
How charged with punishments the scroll,
I am the master of my fate,
I am the captain of my soul.

- *Invictus* by William Ernest Henley

You are the master of your fate, you are the captain of your soul.

The 19th century poet, William Ernest Henley, was suffering from

tuberculosis when he wrote this poem. It's one of the most famous

motivational poems in history. It reminds us that we are the ones

in control of our lives, and we have to cease giving our control

over to external forces. I recite it every day because it reminds me

that I am in control of my own life.

In the past chapters, I talked about taming your mind and controlling it, now we will delve into controlling your fate by dictating it. Your body is your country, it's your earth, it's your domain. In this domain, you have to dictate the law. If you become close-minded, then close-mindedness is the law of your domain; you will not take in the knowledge and help you need to improve your life. If you decide to be cynical, then the law of your domain is cynicism. What laws are you willing to put in place for yourself right now so you can reach your goals?

Think of the laws that govern your country; in my country, The United States Constitution is the law of the land, and for close to three hundred years later, the constitution still oversees millions of citizens as the law of the land in one of the world's biggest and most impactful democracies. So constitutions have the potential to produce huge impacts, why not create your own constitution for yourself?

Draft a constitution where you write the laws and execute them. That's arguably a lot of work, but it will pay dividends for your self-development.

What do you demand of yourself? In your constitution, answer questions like these: Who am I? What do I desire? What is my direction? What makes me different? What are my values and principles? What are my finance laws? What are my relationship laws? What are my work laws?

Make your constitution clear yet flexible so you can interpret it as you go through life's many challenges. Consider how there are conflicts between the interests of people and groups, and these conflicts end up in court because decisions have to be made based on justice and equal representation. But the conflicts under your constitution are going to involve you vs. life; if, in your constitution, you decide that you are going to be a well organized professional, but suddenly you get so busy that you cannot clean up after yourself and your office gets messy, you have a conflict. How will you deal with that conflict? Interpret your constitution the same way a judge is supposed to interpret the constitution

when dealing with a case. In order to keep yourself well

organized, you'll have to be more cognizant of the things you

carelessly throw down and forget to clean. Go back over your

constitution, and abide by it's laws or amend it as you grow.

You're probably thinking, "abiding by and revising my codes or

constitution is fine in theory yet in practice it's hard to stay on

track, it's hard to execute." It can be hard, but this leads to my next

point.

In order to assure that you are actively executing your

constitution, keep it with you. Hang your constitution up in your

room, memorize it, and recite it regularly. The more you recite it,

the more it sticks into your brain and molds you, and the execution

of your constitution becomes second nature.

The execution comes in the form of your actions, it is what

makes you great. You have an overall goal as spelled out in your

constitution, and then you have minor goals that, if practiced

regularly, will lead to your overall goals. For example, if your constitution states that you will read twenty books for the year, then you need to include in your constitution that you will read X amount of words every day in order to reach the twenty books for the year. In order to become great, to set yourself apart from everyone else, you'll have to execute your constitution every day so you can grow a little bit every day.

As you get closer to your goals, you'll need to amend certain laws in your constitution, like your finance laws if you want to go back to school after years of working, or your transportation laws, if you want to switch from a coupe to a minivan. But the essence of your constitution shouldn't change; if your law or code is to provide for your family, then you should do that no matter what amendments you make to your constitution.

Currently, I'm dictating my life. As a child I rebelled a lot because I didn't feel in control. When I went to college, I didn't dictate my life since I didn't discover myself, so I majored in whatever subject I thought would make me a lot of money. When I went into the workforce, I halfway dictated my life because I had economic freedoms, but I wasn't passionate about my work. I really started dictating my life after I discovered myself. That's when I realized that I wanted to be around my family more often and I wanted to start a business where I could help people. Now, I enjoy my work and I am able to work closer to my family, and since this is what I want, I am dictating my life.

In all honesty, it doesn't matter if you are the smartest person or the most privileged person in the world; if you constantly make terrible decisions, then you are a fool and you will be a prisoner of your bad decisions or indecisions. If this is the case, then you are not the master of your fate, you are not the captain of your soul, you are not steering your ship. You must dictate your life by making the decisions that will define you as you want to be defined.

You are already born in this world with a genetic makeup that is the only one of its kind in history. The choices you make in this world will either solidify your unique identity or they will erode it and cast you aside. Your decision to read this book is a decision to improve your life, your decision to abuse drugs is a decision to hurt your life.

So if you want to take control of your life and live passionately, then start dictating it!

29. Divinity

Though we are not Almighty God Himself, nevertheless, we are now divine. - Marcus Tulius Cicero

If there is a level of luck or divinity that helps you along your path to greatness, it is because you put yourself in a position for luck or divine intervention. So, put yourself in a position to be divine.

There is the noun "divine" which is to be godlike, and there is the verb "to divine" which is to discover by intuition. Both are correlated in this chapter; you must follow all 29 D's so you have the necessary understanding of self and experience to be so masterful at your craft that you can *divine* the intricacies of that craft without much thought. In order to *be divine*, you must become so skillful and talented that you do things that an average human being in your field cannot do.

Warren Buffett is divine when he analyzes stocks and makes winning decisions, Tom Brady is divine when he analyzes his opponents and makes a winning play. People who are divine develop a sixth sense for their craft; they know their craft in three dimensions, while everyone else can only see one or two dimensions.

If you saw Super Bowl 50 in 2017, you saw something absolutely great—The New England Patriot's comeback. The Atlanta Falcons were beating The New England Patriots by 25 points with five minutes on the clock in the 3rd quarter. But then the Patriots had what I call a **divine** moment: Tom Brady (their quarterback) threw laser passes to his targets, the defense applied pressure, especially when linebacker Dont'a Hightower strip-sacked The Atlanta Falcons' Quarterback Matt Ryan; Brady's receivers, Amendola and Edelman, among others, made great catches, and the running back, James White, scored the winning touchdown in overtime.

When you are at your worst, it's another opportunity to grow and reach your greatness. When your back is against the wall, the only place to go is forward; when you have fallen into a hole, the only place to go is up. Being divine is being so masterful that you are godlike. In football, Tom Brady is godlike; in running,

Usain Bolt is godlike; in art, Michelangelo is godlike; in business, Richard Branson is godlike; in music, Prince is godlike; and in basketball, MJ is godlike.

Reaching a divine state takes time and effort—every day you will have to work on improving your craft. After years of learning and practicing, the results of your practice can come to light—and you can become a master; you can become divine.

When thinking of divinity, think of people who know their craft inside and out. Bishop Michael V. Talbert once told me, there's a tube that goes from a divine spirit and connects to each human; so in that way, we all have divinity in us, we just have to work on our greatness to bring it out.

Mother Teresa didn't do things half way; she *demanded* change by demanding more from herself.[35] When she went to Calcutta, India, she saw the poverty so many Indians lived in, and she decided to demand more from herself in order to make a difference in their lives. The demands she made for herself

---

[35] Spink, Kathryn. Mother Teresa: an Authorized Biography. HarperOne, 2011.

resulted in an open school for poor children. Soon she gathered

attention from donors. As time went on, she began providing

services all over India, and her efforts led to more funding for

charity work. Now charities across the world have her name

attached to them and follow the *design* she originated. She is great

because of the amount of effort she gave to her work. Her use of

the Ds of Greatness, including her determination, development,

and discipline gave rise to many skills in charity work, like

organization, communication, and compassion among others.

However, Mother Teresa wasn't recognized solely because of her

skills in charity work, but she was recognized because of her

mastery of charity work; in other words, in charity work, Mother

Teresa was divine.

   If you think about it, a combination of the Ds lead people

to reach their greatest potentials, helping them become award

recipients in every field; Nobel Prize Laureates follow the Ds

intimately. These recipients are in the 1% of their fields, they are the divine masters of their fields. The Ds will also lead you to

your divinity.

So if you want to be divine at your craft, follow the Ds of

Greatness.

30. Destiny

Control Your Own Destiny or Someone Else Will - Jack Welch

Don't be an external searcher —someone who runs around from place to place, from person to person, from sensation to sensation searching for "meaning" in life. You'll never find it. External searchers are vulnerable, and vulnerability can easily be exploited by manipulators. Trust me, I see it. I see snake oil salesmen sell people dreams that don't come true, parents force their children to follow paths they don't want, dreamers give up on their dreams, and lovers lose the loves of their lives.

Instead, listen to what's inside of you. Your meaning in life, your destiny, is always inside of you. What interests you? What are you curious to learn more about? That which is inside of you can manifest into greatness if you let it. You may have a lot of creativity or leadership qualities inside of you that you have to mold into greatness through experiences, so acknowledge what qualities you have inside of you and go experience your environment.

Are you destined for greatness? The answer to this question depends on the answer to another question: have you worked towards your own idea of greatness?

Our perception of destiny is flawed; collectively, we watch too many superhero and disney movies to the point where a misunderstanding of "destiny" seeps into our brains and our culture. We think destiny is something that happens naturally, something we have at birth. We think people like Nicola Tesla, George Washington Carver, Jay-Z, Barack Obama, and all those who achieve greatness are destined for greatness in the womb—as if some prophecy was created at their birth, as if a deity blessed them. The truth is less mystical. If a deity blessed these people, it was because they got its attention. If a prophecy was written for them, they authored it. If they were destined for greatness in the womb, it was because the person carrying them brought them into this world with love and support. You are enchanted at birth, your very existence is a testament to your greatness; your life is selected for birth out of trillions of potential lives. Now if you want to become great among those who are blessed with life, you must create your own greatness.

Manifestation

You have greatness inside of you already, all you need to do is let it show, let it materialize in the world we live in. What does this greatness look like? Does it manifest itself in in art? in public service? in inventions? in writing? in teaching? in farming? Whatever it is, let it be unique to you, and let it flow from the inside out.

Your destiny is a matter of your uniqueness, and that's why following the D's in the method I've outlined is so important. In order for you to identify your destiny, you have to begin with discovery—you have to internally search within yourself and find out your likes and dislikes, loves and hates, real culture and fake culture, influencers and followers, and dreams and nightmares. Then when you take this self-discovery and move through the Ds, you'll realize that your destiny has always been inside of you, just waiting to come out.

Never Give Up - Defiance

I knew I was destined for financial success because I was driven to succeed from a young age, and whenever I made a sale as a kid, whether it was selling candy or jewelry, it made me happy. So I constantly sold, and I never gave up. Even when I started selling stocks, I never gave up on a prospect. When Jay-Z was questioned on his success and genius, he said, "The most genius thing we ever did was never give up."[36] You can control your destiny by your actions, and an extremely important part of destiny is to **never give up**. If you can define yourself as defiant, then you are increasing the likelihood that one of your attempts at success will work!

Your destiny is not given to you, it is something that you must write for yourself through introspection, defiance, and the revelation of your internal world into the external world around you. The Ds will help you reveal your destiny, but you'll have to look inside to find it!

---

[36] //www.forbes.com/sites/bruceupbin/. "Jay-Z, Buffett and Forbes on Success and Giving Back." *Forbes*, Forbes Magazine, 23 Sept. 2010, www.forbes.com/forbes/2010/1011/rich-list-10-omaha-warren-buffett-jay-z-steve-forbes-summit-interview.html. Accessed 24 Sept. 2017.

Index

Made in the USA
Middletown, DE
05 October 2021